The Art of Positive Communication

This book is part of the Peter Lang Media and Communication list.
Every volume is peer reviewed and meets
the highest quality standards for content and production.

PETER LANG
New York • Bern • Frankfurt • Berlin
Brussels • Vienna • Oxford • Warsaw

JULIEN C. MIRIVEL

The Art of Positive Communication

THEORY AND PRACTICE

PETER LANG
New York • Bern • Frankfurt • Berlin
Brussels • Vienna • Oxford • Warsaw

Library of Congress Cataloging-in-Publication Data

Mirivel, Julien C.
The art of positive communication: theory and practice / Julien C. Mirivel.
pages cm
Includes bibliographical references and index.
1. Interpersonal communication. 2. Social interaction. I. Title.
HM1166.M57   302—dc23   2014016401
ISBN 978-1-4331-2100-5 (hardcover)
ISBN 978-1-4331-2099-2 (paperback)
ISBN 978-1-4539-1383-3 (e-book)

Bibliographic information published by **Die Deutsche Nationalbibliothek**.
Die Deutsche Nationalbibliothek lists this publication in the "Deutsche
Nationalbibliografie"; detailed bibliographic data are available
on the Internet at http://dnb.d-nb.de/.

Cover image by Annick Vauthier
www.annickvauthier.ch

The paper in this book meets the guidelines for permanence and durability
of the Committee on Production Guidelines for Book Longevity
of the Council of Library Resources.

© 2014 Peter Lang Publishing, Inc., New York
29 Broadway, 18th floor, New York, NY 10006
www.peterlang.com

Printed in the United States of America

TABLE OF CONTENTS

Acknowledgments   ix

Chapter 1: Introduction   1
   The Context   2
   The Purpose   4
   The Model of Positive Communication   7
   Overview   10
   Summary   12
   Further Reading   13
   Key Conceptual and Theoretical Terms   13

Chapter 2: Positive Communication Creates Contact   15
   Prelude   15
   Introduction   16
   Theoretical Knowledge   17
      The Constitutive View of Communication   18
      Speech Act Theory   19
      Conversation Analysis   24
   Practical Knowledge   29
      Greeting as Positive Communication   30

Summary   33
Further Reading   33
Key Conceptual and Theoretical Terms   34

Chapter 3: Positive Communication Discovers the Unknown   35
Prelude   35
Introduction   36
Theoretical Knowledge   37
    Coordinated Management of Meaning Theory   37
    Forms of Questioning   39
Practical Knowledge   52
    Asking as Positive Communication   52
Summary   55
Further Reading   56
Key Conceptual and Theoretical Terms   56

Chapter 4: Positive Communication Affects the Self   57
Prelude   57
Introduction   58
Theoretical Knowledge   59
    Symbolic Interactionism   59
    Altercasting   60
    Ossification   63
    Intertextuality and Authoring   67
Practical Knowledge   71
    Complimenting as Positive Communication   71
Summary   76
Further Reading   76
Key Conceptual and Theoretical Terms   76

Chapter 5: Positive Communication Deepens Relationship   79
Prelude   79
Introduction   80
Theoretical Knowledge   80
    Three Theories of Disclosure   81
    Forms of Disclosure   84
Practical Knowledge   90
    Disclosing as Positive Communication   90
    Directions for Turning Point Graph   93
Summary   94
Further Reading   95

Key Conceptual and Theoretical Terms   95

Chapter 6: Positive Communication Gives Support   97
    Prelude   97
    Introduction   98
    Theoretical Knowledge   98
        Instrumental Support   100
        Emotional Support   104
        Esteem Support   108
    Practical Knowledge   111
        Encouraging as Positive Communication   111
    Summary   115
    Further Reading   115
    Key Conceptual and Theoretical Terms   116

Chapter 7: Positive Communication Transcends Separateness   117
    Prelude   117
    Introduction   117
    Theoretical Knowledge   118
        Dialogue and Dialogic Communication   119
    Practical Knowledge   129
        Listening as Positive Communication   129
    Summary   135
    Further Reading   135
    Key Conceptual and Theoretical Terms   136

Chapter 8: Positive Communication Influences Others   137
    Prelude   137
    Introduction   138
    Theoretical Knowledge   138
        Communication Accommodation Theory   139
        Positive Deviance Approach   144
        Virtue Ethics and Communication Excellence   147
    Practical Knowledge   150
        Inspiring as Positive Communication   150
    Summary   156
    Further Reading   156
    Key Conceptual and Theoretical Terms   157

Chapter 9: Conclusion   159
    Prelude   159

Introduction   160
The Model of Positive Communication   161
  Greet and Create   162
  Ask and Discover   162
  Compliment and Affect   163
  Disclose and Deepen   163
  Encourage and Give   164
  Listen and Transcend   164
  Inspire and Influence   165
Communication Is a Creative Art   166
Summary   169
Further Reading   170
Key Conceptual and Theoretical Terms   170

References   171

Index   187

ACKNOWLEDGMENTS

This book was made possible by the support of many individuals. First, I am grateful for Mary Savigar at Peter Lang who saw potential in the proposal and enabled this book to come to life. Second, I am indebted to the anonymous reviewer whose comments elevated the manuscript and my thinking to a new level; I am truly grateful. Thanks also to the production team at Peter Lang for their outstanding work on the final details. Finally, many family members, mentors, colleagues, and friends made a special difference. For this project, I want to especially thank Karen Tracy for her feedback on the original draft, Rob Ulmer for his advice throughout the process, and Alexander Lyon for believing in the project and encouraging me along the way. Thanks also to Joe Williams for being a constant source of friendship on and off the tennis court. Finally, my deepest gratitude is to Meg and my son Hugo. Thank you, Meg, for editing this work and for listening, and for your love and support. And, of course, to Hugo who inspires me to practice what I teach.

· 1 ·

INTRODUCTION

"The spoken word, spoken honorably and well, can make a difference that no other form of communication can equal."

—MARVIN JENSEN

George Vaillant has been directing the Harvard Grant Study for more than 40 years. The project is one of the most significant longitudinal studies of adult development ever conducted. Since 1938, scholars and scientists have interviewed, surveyed, and collected data on 268 individuals starting when they were 19 years old. The study has followed these persons for 75 years, many of whom are now well into their 90s. In one interview, Vaillant was asked what the most significant finding from the 75-year study was. His response was immediate: "The only thing that really matters in life are your relationships with other people" (Vaillant, 2012, p. 27). "Happiness is love. Full stop" (p. 52).

There is no doubt that the relationships we have with people around us matter. As Vaillant (2012) wrote, "Throughout our lives we are shaped and enriched by the sustaining surround of our relationships" (p. 52). Warm relationships between parent and child have long-lasting consequences; so do each person's ability to sustain meaningful friendships or a healthy marriage. The ability to create warm connections is simply critical to leading a happy and fulfilling life. This point is well-echoed in the words of the thinker Jiddu Krishnamurti (1992), who said, "Life is relationship; to be is to be related."

Even with the understanding that relationships matter, important questions remain: How can people create warm relationships? What defining behaviors lead to the development of healthy marriages? Of lifelong friendships? Or of meaningful sibling relationships? Relationships do not simply exist on their own. They are not "warm," "cold," "close," or "distant" on the basis of conditions beyond human control. Instead, as I will show throughout this book, all relationships are created by communication. It is the way people communicate that cultivates the nature of their relationship. Healthy, productive, and meaningful communication can lead to healthy, productive, and meaningful relationships. This book provides a road map for how you can communicate better to create enhanced relationships with others.

This book is a practical guide for communication students who want to communicate more positively. Its major purpose is to strengthen your ability to communicate with others. In this book, I propose that practicing positive communication will help you grow as a person, improve the quality of the relationships in your life, and cultivate communication as a social practice. To do so, this book introduces a model of positive communication to guide communicative conduct. The model is informed by theory and research in the field of interpersonal communication and language and social interaction. In this chapter, I first contextualize the book in light of the recent positive movement in the field of interpersonal communication. Then, I explain the main purpose of the book and what it seeks to accomplish. The third major section defines positive communication and introduces a model of positive communication that provides the major framework for this text. In the conclusion, I overview the main chapters and invite you to reflect about the importance of communicating positively.

The Context

This book is written within the larger frame of two areas of study in the field of communication: Interpersonal Communication and Language and Social Interaction. **Interpersonal Communication** (capitalized) simply refers to a body of scholarship that examines personal and social relationships and the important role that communication plays in those relationships (see Knapp & Daly, 2011). Researchers who study interpersonal communication explore a wide variety of topics such as the way personality affects communication between people (see Daly, 2011), the way supportive communication takes place in family relationships (e.g., see MacGeorge, Feng, & Burleson, 2011), or the strategies couples use during conflict (see Roloff & Chiles, 2011). This book especially draws on important research on **interpersonal skills**, or the behaviors that constitute competency in everyday interaction (see, e.g., Spitzberg & Cupach, 2011).

This book also is informed by scholarship in Language and Social Interaction (see Fitch & Sanders, 2005). **Language and Social Interaction** is the name used to describe a body of research that explores the way people use verbal or nonverbal behaviors in naturally occurring interaction. Traditionally, researchers in Language and Social Interaction audio- or video-record human interaction in a real context at home or at work, transcribe what people said and/or did during the conversation, and analyze the communication to reveal something interesting about what is taking place. Research in this area has analyzed the way people use compliments in everyday talk (see Pomerantz, 1978), how socialization takes place during family dinners (see Blum-Kulka, 1997), how communication problems emerge during 911 phone calls (Tracy & Tracy, 1998), how FBI negotiations unfold (Agne & Tracy, 2001), or even how cosmetic surgeons sell surgery to new clients (Mirivel, 2008). Typically, researchers in Language and Social Interaction reveal the mechanisms that operate in conversations (e.g., Conversation Analysis), the important functions that certain forms of talk or visible actions serve (see Streeck, Goodwin, & LeBaron, 2011), or how racism is perpetuated in everyday talk (van Dijk, 1997). Together, these two areas of study offer a wealth of information about how, what, and why people communicate as they do in romantic relationships, in friendships, in families, or in professional environments.

This book especially focuses on the positive side of interpersonal communication. Historically, the fields of Interpersonal Communication and Language and Social Interaction have both focused on the dark side of communication, its problematic or dilemmatic nature, or the communication challenges that people face in relationships. In Interpersonal Communication, this is well-displayed in an iconic volume by Cupach and Spitzberg (2007) titled *The Dark Side of Interpersonal Communication*. Researchers have sought to understand the nature of hurtful messages (Vangelisti, 2007), the nature of revenge (Yoshimura, 2007), aggression (Dailey, Lee, & Spitzberg, 2007), or abuse (Morgan & Wilson, 2007). Even in Language and Social Interaction, there is a tendency for scholars to focus on the problematic nature of human interaction. Researchers, for example, have analyzed how a conflict emerged between George W. Bush and the journalist Dan Rather during a

CBS interview (e.g., Pomerantz, 1988; Schegloff, 1988), how hostility is used during public meetings (Tracy, 2008), or how patients pressure physicians for medications (Gill, 2005).

In spite of these tendencies, there is a burgeoning focus on the positive side of interpersonal communication. This movement first emerged in psychology with Seligman's (2002) work on the nature of personal happiness, Peterson and Seligman's (2004) scientific work on virtues such as courage or compassion, and Csikszentmihalyi's (1990) study of optimal experience and flow. In communication, the positive focus is pioneered by Socha and Pitts (2012a, 2012b). In *The Positive Side of Interpersonal Communication*, for example, the authors brought together communication researchers to provide a conceptual foundation of the positive side of interpersonal communication. In the volume, various authors discuss the nature of excellence (Mirivel, 2012), the importance of intimacy (Nussbaum, Miller-Day, & Fisher, 2012), how friends play (Aune & Wong, 2012), as well as review the research on forgiveness (Kelley, 2012) and supportive communication (MacGeorge, Feng, Wilkum, & Doherty, 2012). Socha and Pitts's volume thus provides a foundation for understanding what people do well when they communicate, how positive communication can be enacted, and how positive communication behaviors can help create healthy relationships. However, there is no text in the field that introduces positive communication to students.

This book is informed by research in Interpersonal Communication and Language and Social Interaction. It also joins a disciplinary focus on the positive side of communication. The objective of this book, however, is not to simply share what researchers know about positive communication. This book was written to enable you to practice communication more positively. In the next section, I describe this purpose more carefully and explain how the book will accomplish it.

The Purpose

The focus of the book is on the practice of interpersonal communication. Defined simply, interpersonal communication refers to the process of engaging in communication with another person. As Baxter and Braithwaite (2008) explained, "Most scholars agree that interpersonal communication 'is a process; involves a dyad or normally a small number of people; it involves creating meanings; and it is enacted through verbal and nonverbal message behaviors'" (p. 6). In sum, then, **interpersonal communication** (not capitalized) is the process through which two or more people create meaning through verbal and nonverbal communication.

Everyone engages in interpersonal communication. We talk with our family members, catch up with our friends, or laugh with our colleagues. We each spend a significant amount of time interacting with others, learning with or through them, and managing our relationships with others. With time, then, every adult builds a tremendous amount of experience in the practice of interpersonal communication. Through the process of interpersonal communication, we develop our personal communication style; we learn to manage conflict in a particular way, and we develop specific habits. Every event that you have experienced, every conversation that you have been a part of, and every encounter with others that you have had form your personal **field of experience**. Your field of experience also includes moments of communication that you have witnessed, heard about, or read about. It includes all of the information that you have gathered throughout your life to make sense of, and practice, communication. In sum, when you communicate, you draw on and build your own field of experience. This field of experience, however, may not reflect the latest research available in communication, an understanding of key concepts or theories, or even the scientific methods for analyzing a conversation. By providing new information about communication, this book will thus deepen your field of experience.

The major purpose of this book is to strengthen the way you communicate. Improving one's communication is not easy. Some scholars even argue that a person's communication style seldom fluctuates (see Cegala, 1981; McCroskey, 1984). Researchers have explained that communicating well requires motivation, knowledge, and skills (Spitzberg, 1983). For this book, I assume that you are motivated to communicate better, that you want to learn more about the topic and improve the way you engage in the practice of communication. I also assume that you join the reading of this text with already existing communication skills; that is, you have the ability to perform "situationally appropriate behavior" (Spitzberg, 1983, p. 323) in many contexts and situations. Finally, I assume that you already have much knowledge about how to enact communication in a variety of contexts.

However, there is still much to be learned: positive communication is an art for a lifetime. Communication scholars and students, in fact, can "benefit from understanding communication as a verbal (and nonverbal) art" (Baxter, Norwood, & Nebel, 2012, p. 19). And like any other art, such as painting, sculpting, or writing, positive communication is an art that requires mastering theory and practice. As Fromm (1956) explained, "the process of learning an art can be divided conveniently into two parts: one, the master of the theory; the other, the mastery of the practice" (p. 5). This book is designed with this point in mind. First, this book will expand your **theoretical knowledge** of communication by introducing core concepts and major communication theories to enable you to make sense of everyday human interaction in more sophisticated ways. Second, the book will expand your **practical knowledge** of positive communication. Every chapter, in fact, is built around this core structure. The first part of each chapter will focus on theoretical knowledge and the second part will focus on practical knowledge. By attending to both theory and practice, you will thus strengthen your ability to practice positive communication and develop mastery of communication as an art.

Learning to communicate positively is important. It has a range of positive consequences. Communication skills, for example, are crucial in the professional world. Employers consistently rank verbal and written communication in the top of what they look for in potential employees. Communicating positively can foster your happiness and help you cope with stress and adversity. Positive communication also improves a person's physical and psychological health and can enable you to self-actualize, to nudge you toward your potential as a person. As Karen Lebacqz (1985) wrote, "When we act, we not only do something, we also shape our own character. Our choices about what to do are also choices about whom to be or, more accurately, whom to become" (p. 83). Positive communication has a range of tangible, practical outcomes.

Learning to communicate positively also matters because you affect others and your relationships with people all around you, including those you care deeply about and love. Friendships, romantic relationships, and family life are all created by the way people communicate with one another. As Virginia Satir (1976) wrote in *Making Contact*, "Communication is to relationship what breathing is to maintaining life." Without communication, it is impossible to have or maintain a relationship with anyone. A gaze, a gesture, a wink, stepping in closer, a touch on the shoulder, and what we say or do not say all contribute to the way we "do" relationship. Communication is relationship. Relationships are not things we have, but things that we do through communication. We are thus constantly relating with people around us. The choice is not whether to have a relationship, but in what way: Close or distant? Warm or cold? Surface or deep? Negative or positive?

The way we communicate matters beyond our self and the relationships we care about. By practicing communication in a particular direction, we are also inherently cultivating in our society the practices that we believe are important (see Craig, 2006). Our personal communication helps these practices survive in our community. To use an analogy, if you sit down to eat dinner with your family every night instead of watching television, you are sustaining a practice that you believe matters; then, your children will learn from this and grow to do the same. Communication is a practice, too, and our everyday actions cultivate that practice in our society. Positive communication is a choice that keeps important ways of speaking and doing alive in the culture of which we are part.

In sum, the purpose of this book is to increase your theoretical knowledge and practical knowledge of positive communication. After reading this book, you will be able to explain the nature of positive communication, describe various theoretical frameworks to make sense of human interaction, and practice positive communication more frequently in your life. With this purpose in mind, I now define positive communication and introduce the model of positive communication that is grounding the book.

The Model of Positive Communication

Positive communication refers to any verbal and nonverbal behaviors that function positively in the course of human interaction. It includes all of the "communicative processes and forms which we would be proud to model and teach to children" (Socha & Pitts, 2012a, p. 324). Positive communication reflects our potential: what we are capable of doing. It includes all of the behaviors that reflect our best, that produce personal and relational happiness and satisfaction, as well as those that challenge our self to move in the direction of others and to act ethically.

This book focuses on seven behaviors that exemplify positive communication. These communicative practices include greeting, asking, complimenting, disclosing, encouraging, listening, and inspiring. There are other behaviors that will qualify as positive communication. For example, playing or joking could be included as important behaviors that illustrate positive communication. I am not suggesting here that these behaviors do not exemplify positive communication or that there are not others that would not qualify. Instead, my position is that these seven behaviors are fundamental to the practice of positive communication. First, they are a good starting point to guide reflection, inquiry, and engagement in positive communication. Second, there is much empirical and scientific research to document the value of each behavior in cultivating human relationships. Third, they are easy to remember, practice, and experiment with in everyday life. Fourth, each behavior reflects a counterpoint to certain interactional tendencies. For example, complimenting is a counter-choice to the tendency to criticize. Disclosing is the counter-choice to the tendency to conceal information. In summary, these seven communication behaviors exemplify positive communication as a practice. They are illustrated in this **Model of Positive Communication** (Figure 1.1).

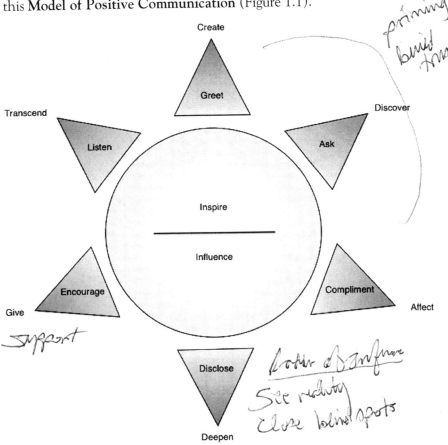

Figure 1.1. Model of Positive Communication.

The Model of Positive Communication is a descriptive and normative model. It is descriptive because it illustrates communication behaviors that exemplify positive communication as a practice and the important functions of these communication behaviors. According to the model, for example, greetings serve multiple functions, but a primary one is to create contact. Asking questions enables each of us to discover others. Compliments often affect a person's

development and growth. Disclosing deepens relationships. Encourag
support to those in need. Listening allows speakers to transcend the
ences. And inspiring has the power to influence. The seven behaviors are thus
encompassed in the following core principles of positive communication:

1. Greeting creates contact.
2. Asking discovers the unknown.
3. Complimenting affects the development of self.
4. Disclosing deepens relationships.
5. Encouraging gives support.
6. Listening transcends human separateness.
7. Inspiring influences others.

These principles, and their related positive communication behavior, offer
a guide for understanding how positive communication functions in human
interaction.

In addition to describing the nature of positive communication, the model
also is normative. It proposes that these communicative behaviors should be
practiced. Greeting, asking, complimenting, disclosing, encouraging, listening,
and inspiring are behaviors that students of human communication should
enact in their everyday interaction. As I will illustrate herein, these behaviors
foster quality human relationships, create positive organizational cultures, and
help to cultivate in our society forms of human communication that reflect our
best. It is important to note here that the model is not suggesting that these
behaviors should be enacted at all times or that they are "laws" to direct behavior. Every context and every interaction are unique moments in time that
are shaped by local contingencies, individual personalities, and relational his-
tories. The model is not a system of law; it is a guide for action. It serves as an
encouragement to choose behaviors that may sometimes be counterintuitive
or difficult to perform under pressure. My hope is that the model is a reminder
to practice positive communication whenever it is possible. But good communication is not about following a simple recipe; it is about choosing to respond
with creativity and love.

Finally, the model provides an organizing framework for positive communication research and promotes further inquiry about positive communication.
Traditionally, research in the field of communication is organized by contexts
of study or traditions of thought (see Craig, 1999). For example, researchers
focus on interpersonal communication, organizational communication, group
communication, or crisis communication. This model suggests that research

on positive communication could be organized around the behaviors that constitute it rather than the contexts in which they occur. Researchers can thus foster an understanding of a given behavior across contexts: How are greetings used in personal relationships? What functions do they serve in the workplace? How do they operate in medical interaction? What about encouraging as a form of positive communication? How does encouraging take place in the legal context or as part of leadership? With questions in mind, researchers could explore the impact of positive communication behaviors across contexts and cultivate an understanding of the practice of positive communication.

For students, the model can guide inquiry and the development of small-scale research projects about positive communication. The model can and should be challenged. But it can also be used as a tool for discovery. Students can develop research questions related to the model, collect data, and discover if the findings align or do not align with the model. In fact, every chapter in this text describes a small-scale project to help students seek and discover on their own the value of the behaviors that are introduced. My hope is that these projects can serve as seeds for students to develop larger research projects on positive communication in the future.

Positive communication refers to verbal and nonverbal messages that function positively in the course of human interaction. This book introduces the Model of Positive Communication to explain the nature of positive communication and to practice it in everyday life. In the next section, I overview the chapters in the book and conclude.

Overview

The major purpose of this book is to strengthen the way you communicate. With this purpose in mind, every chapter is structured with two major sections: a theoretical knowledge section and a practical knowledge section. In the theoretical knowledge section, I describe relevant communication theory and concepts to support the principle. In the practical knowledge section, I invite you to engage in three major activities: reflect, study, and practice the focal behavior that is relevant for the chapter. The reflection activities are designed to explore your experience and thinking about positive communication. The study activities offer small-scale projects to understand positive communication viewed from the perspectives of others. The practice activities are designed to encourage you to enact each positive communication behavior in everyday life.

In Chapter 2, I draw on the constitutive model of communication, speech act theory, and conversation analysis to show that communication creates contact; it is a process through which people create meaning together. The positive communication behavior that exemplifies this principle best is our ability to greet. Greetings are incredibly important in human interaction and initiating greeting moves us in the direction of others and begins the process of relating.

Chapter 3 introduces the second principle: Asking discovers the unknown. People get to know one another and manage their relationships by asking questions and providing answers. The questions we ask one another are thus crucial. In the chapter, I introduce Coordinated Management of Meaning theory and the distinction between closed-ended questions and open-ended questions. I argue that open-ended questions promote the process of discovery and function positively in human interaction. The chapter then invites you to ask more questions to discover others.

In Chapter 4, the focus is on the way we affect each other through communication. The principle is that communication affects the self. I review a theory called Symbolic Interactionism to explain that every person's sense of self is affected by what other people say to them. Through communication, people altercast one another, ossify each other, and become intertextualized. And yet, we have the ability to make communicative choices that make a positive difference in the lives of others. One important way of affecting others positively is to compliment them, even though sometimes our impulse is to criticize. By focusing on the positive, we can strengthen one another.

Chapter 5 is a reflection on the process of disclosure. It is driven by the argument that disclosing deepens relationship. In the chapter, I draw on three major theories: Social Penetration Theory, Relational Dialectics, and Communication Boundary Management Theory. With these theories, the chapter shows that revealing ourselves is a challenge in part because it moves us closer to the people we love. But without disclosure, it is impossible to create intimacy and to sustain those relationships. This is one reason why this chapter encourages you to disclose.

In Chapter 6, I argue that communication gives meaning to our lives. The chapter reviews the theoretical work on social support to show that positive communication is an act of giving. Specifically, we can give each other (a) comfort, (b) support, and (c) affection. As Comte-Sponville (2001) wrote, "no one is the cause of himself or, in the end, of his own joy" (p. 134). In this sense, we can give each other the courage to be. And there is no better way to do it than by encouraging.

Positive communication transcends human separateness. Chapter 7 explores this sixth principle. Every person is a unique being, but human beings are more similar than they are different. Communication is a process through which people can transcend their differences. When these moments occur, scholars call them "dialogic moments" because they involve human beings experiencing one another fully for brief moments in time. Often, these moments of synergy are created by people who are willing and able to suspend judgment, be open to others and their perspective, have empathy, and be authentic and genuine. But listening deeply to others is the most effective way of transcending our perceived differences.

Principle seven states that communication influences others. Chapter 8 supports this principle by reviewing three major theoretical frameworks: (a) Communication Accommodation Theory, (b) the Positive Deviance approach, and (c) Virtue Ethics. Together, these theories show that when we communicate, we have choices about how to be or whom to become, and that positive communication can begin a wave of influence. The last positive communication behavior encompasses them all: The best way to influence others is to inspire.

In the conclusion, I review the Model of Positive Communication and invite you to create communication rituals that will strengthen your relationships. Positive communication is about making choices that move beyond our automatic response system. Being able to do so requires theory, practice, and creativity.

Summary

Positive communication is a relatively new area of study in the field of communication. For the most part, communication scholars have focused on the problematic nature of human interaction and its dark side. This is unfortunate. Communication students need to see how people interact when they are at their best, what positive communication is, and what principles of communicative conduct should ground its practice. This book will give you the theoretical and practical knowledge to understand, study, and practice positive communication. More importantly, it will enable you to make better human contact with others and to enjoy even more the moments of human communication that create your life.

Further Reading

Craig, R. T. (1999). Communication theory as a field. *Communication Theory, 9,* 119–161.

Cupach, W. R., & Spitzberg, B. H. (Eds.). (2007). *The dark side of interpersonal communication.* Mahwah, NJ: Erlbaum.

Fromm, E. (1956). *The art of loving.* New York: Harper Collins.

Knapp, M. L., & Daly, J. A. (Eds.) (2002). *Handbook of interpersonal communication.* Thousand Oaks, CA: Sage.

Satir, V. (1976). *Making contact.* Ann Arbor, MI: University of Michigan Press.

Socha, T. J., & Pitts, M. J. (Eds.) (2012). *The positive side of interpersonal communication.* New York: Peter Lang.

Vaillant, G. E. (2012). *Triumphs of experience: The men of the Harvard Grant Study.* Cambridge, MA: Belknap Press.

Key Conceptual and Theoretical Terms

Interpersonal Communication
interpersonal skills
Language and Social Interaction
interpersonal communication
field of experience
theoretical knowledge
practical knowledge
positive communication
Model of Positive Communication

· 2 ·

POSITIVE COMMUNICATION
CREATES CONTACT

Prelude

A professor travels to Japan to study martial arts with a Grand Master. Upon meeting him, and as he joins the class, the professor immediately displays his abilities and mastery of various techniques. He works hard to make visible all that he knows. In silence, the Grand Master simply observes his performance. After class, the Grand Master invites the student to drink tea in a beautiful garden: "Why don't you join me outside for tea?" he asks politely. After sitting down, the Grand Master slowly pours tea into the cup. Soon, the tea starts to overflow, but the Grand Master continues to pour tea in the cup. Upon this sight, the professor clinches his lips to avoid being rude. But the Grand Master presses on; tea is spilling everywhere. The professor finally loses his patience and says, "the cup is full, no more will go in!" The Grand Master places the teapot down and faces him: "Like this cup, you are full of your own opinions and speculations. How can I show you Zen unless you first empty your cup" (Hyams, 1979, p. 11).

You join this book with a tremendous amount of experience as a communicator. Since you were born, you have participated in a myriad of encounters with others. You have learned to imitate the people in your life and to reenact the culture of which you are part. You also have learned to handle conflict in a particular way, acquired your own conversational style, and use gestures and touch according to existing social norms. Your mother, father, family and friends, and all of the people that you have met in your life have affected your development as a person. In addition, you live in what some scholars see as "a communication intensive culture" (see Cameron, 2001) in which there are many ideas about how to communicate. To put it simply, you are joining this book with many assumptions and ideas about communication. Perhaps, then, it might be good to empty your cup, start anew, and be open to new possibilities.

Introduction

"The main function of conversation is not to get things accomplished, but to improve the quality of experience."
—MIHALI CSIKSZENTMIHALYI, 1990, P. 129

When two Tuareg men see each other in the solitude of the Sahara desert, they prepare for their greeting hours before they meet. Atop their camel, they look across the sand dunes to evaluate from afar the potential threat of the upcoming rider. Their gaze is well trained. They learn with experience to identify the rider, interpret the village the rider comes from or the local tribe the rider belongs to, by analyzing subtle cues. They look for the type of camel the other is riding, the type of saddle being used, the way the person sits on the camel and rides it, and, when they get closer, the shape and form of the veil that is being worn. These cues enable the Tuareg men to protect their lives and to make peaceful contact.

Once the two men meet, one person initiates the greeting. The person who makes the first move depends largely on his status, age, and sex. The first utterance is "*salamu aleykum*," which means "Peace be on you." The other person reciprocates with "*aleykum salam*" (Peace be with you also). Then, the first speaker asks a series of questions starting with, "What do you look like?" This is followed by "Only peace (praise be to Allah)" and "May he do good and well for you." The greeting then leads to other important questions:

"What has gone wrong?," "What bad has occurred?," or "Where does travel take you?" Since there is a real possibility of death, questions about unusual noticings or potential problems help the Tuareg men stay alive (see Youssouf, Grimshaw, & Bird, 1976).

Greetings in the Sahara desert are unique, but they reflect the nature of human communication everywhere. In all cultures, people begin their interaction by greeting one another (Duranti, 1997). In India, it is *"namaste"* (literally meaning "I bow to you"). In France, each person says *"bonjour"* ("good day") paired with a few kisses on the cheeks. In Brazil, it is *"bom dia"* and in China *"ni hao."* Greetings are so important that "people can know each other for 35 years, talk to each other every day, and nonetheless greet each other when they begin a conversation" (Sacks, 1992, p. 97). The reasons why we greet one another are complex, but one important function of a greeting is to acknowledge that another person exists and to make contact. We speak to move in the direction of another, to recognize the other's existence, and to include the other, if only momentarily, in our lives.

In this chapter, I argue that positive communication creates contact. People communicate to create their social worlds—their identities, their relationships, and the culture in which they live. In this chapter, I focus on this principle and introduce greeting as an example of positive communication. In the first part of the chapter, I provide the theoretical background of this principle. In the second part of the chapter, I focus on the practice of greetings and provide a reflection exercise, a short study to conduct, and a few greetings to master.

Theoretical Knowledge

In this section, I provide theoretical background to support the principle that positive communication creates contact. The focus is on understanding that communication is more than exchanging information; our verbal and non-verbal actions create meaning, our identities, the nature of our relationships with others, and the social realities of which we are a part, as well as the social system in which we operate. This view is supported by what communication scholars call the constitutive view of communication. First, I introduce the constitutive view of communication. Then, I draw on two theories to illustrate this point further: Speech Act Theory and Conversation Analysis.

The Constitutive View of Communication

Since at least the late 1940s, communication scholars have thought about communication through the lens of a model called the **transmission model of communication** (e.g., Craig, 1999). Viewed from this perspective, when people communicate, they simply exchange information. One person develops a message and sends it to another person. Once the message is received, the other person gives feedback to complete the cycle. This way of thinking about communication is helpful because it explains some of the common problems that people face in human communication. For example, the model shows that one common problem between people is the way a person designs his or her message. The model also suggests that communication can be affected by external noises such as sounds or internal noises such as thoughts. Furthermore, the transmission model emphasizes that giving feedback is crucial to close the communication loop. Because of these understandings, the transmission model of communication has been deeply influential; most people, professionals and laypersons alike often inherently think about communication as the transmission of information. But communication is more than the exchange of information. It is a process of creation.

The principle that positive communication creates contact is grounded in what communication scholars have called the **constitutive view of communication**. From this perspective, communication is defined as a "constitutive process that produces and reproduces shared meaning" (Craig, 1999, p. 125). Viewed from this perspective, "communication is a primary means whereby social realities, cultural contexts, and the meanings of messages are interactively accomplished and experienced" (Glenn, LeBaron, & Mandelbaum, 2003, p. 21). The constitutive view emphasizes that the act of speaking brings something into existence. People communicate to create their identities, their relationships, their families, and the culture of which they are part. Speaking or gesturing, then, is an act of creation.

To further explain that our communicative behaviors create meaning, I now draw on two theories and their core concepts. My focus is on the notion of what gets done when we speak. I use the term *utterance* to describe the way we speak to each other. An **utterance** is simply a segment of talk such as "How are you?," "Buenos dias," or "I had a great weekend with my family." In the rest of this chapter, I describe how our utterances, or what we say to each other, serve multiple functions, create a unique context for interaction, and have consequences beyond themselves.

Speech Act Theory

"People know what they do; they frequently know why they do what they do; but what they don't know is what what they do does."
—MICHEL FOUCAULT (QTD. IN DREYFUS & RABINOW, 1982, P. 187)

One afternoon, my father and I were driving from Switzerland to France to spend the weekend. The radio was playing softly in the background while we were talking together. At one point during our conversation, a song I liked came on the radio. So, I said to my father: "I really like this song." Immediately, he turned the volume up. How was he able to interpret my utterance as a request?

People understand each other because of multiple codes of meaning that are embedded in language use. First, we rely on the **semantic meaning** of words. The semantic meaning of a word is simply its definition or its lexical meaning. To understand my utterance "I really like this song," my father must know the semantic meaning of each word. Without a vocabulary, it would be difficult to understand another person; this is exactly what happens to us when we travel abroad and do not speak the local language. Second, my utterance is meaningful to my father because the utterance has a **syntactic meaning**. Syntax typically refers to the underlying structure and order of the words in a given sentence. If, for example, I said, "Song I really like this," he would be rather confused. So what gives meaning to an utterance are both the meaning of each word and the ways the words are organized together. There is a third layer that gives meaning to my utterance. My utterance is not simply designed to express my liking of the song, but it also functions as a request to turn the volume up. This is called the **pragmatic meaning** of an utterance. With these three codes of meaning, people can accomplish mutual understanding. This section focuses on this third layer of meaning.

The constitutive view of communication emphasizes that the act of communication is not just designed to exchange information. Instead, when people communicate, their communicative actions serve one or more pragmatic functions. This idea comes from **Speech Act Theory**, a theory that emerged out of the work of the language philosophers John Austin (1962) and John Searle (1969, 1979). At its essence, the theory highlights that we use words to do things. Speaking is an action that serves pragmatic functions. This is why Speech Act Theorists use the term *speech act* to describe the spoken word. Defined simply, a **speech act** is the "social meaning of a short segment of talk"

(Tracy, 2002, p. 64). The lesson of the concept, as illustrated in Table 2.1, is that utterances serve one or more functions.

Table 2.1. Speech Acts Serve Functions.

Speech Act	Possible Function(s)
"Good morning!"	To greet, acknowledge, and/or show respect
"You are simply beautiful."	To express love, affection, and/or compliment
"Did you take the garbage outside?"	To reproach, seek an account, and/or request action
"I am sorry."	To apologize, express remorse, and/or end a conflict
"Don't give up, stay strong."	To encourage, show support, and/or mentor

In his work, John Austin argued that there are as many speech acts as there are verbs. Our utterances can thus be used to encourage, compliment, insult, criticize, praise, greet, or listen. Of importance is that the function(s) of an utterance is grounded in the moment; it is affected by the nature of the interaction, the previous turns of talk, the context surrounding the interaction, and what people are doing together. In one moment, a speech act could function as an insult, and the next it could function as a way to create camaraderie (e.g., Kehily & Nayak, 1997). The function(s) of a speech act is thus largely dependent on what a person is accomplishing when it is produced.

Researchers have shown that even little particles of talk perform one or more function(s). Utterances such as "uh" and "umm," for example, mark that a person is having difficulty or can be used to cue seriousness when delivering bad news. The words "I think" can be used to express a doubt, to avoid being seen as making a commitment to an idea or a claim, to speak less assertively, or to manage group discussion (Craig & Sanusi, 2003). The utterance "oh" is often used to show that the previous utterance is newsworthy to a speaker, as in "Oh, wow, I can't believe that you just got married." Researchers also have examined how people use the sound "mm" when people are eating. In one function, people can mark that the meal is enjoyable such as "Mm, that was a nice quiche. I like that" (Wiggins, 2001, p. 454). In other moments, people use "mm" to compliment the cook, to participate actively in the conversation while eating, but also to avoid participating in a touchy conversation or to prevent an emergent conflict (see Wiggins, 2002). To put it simply, the small words and sounds we use serve key functions in human interaction.

Greetings are speech acts that serve important functions. We use greetings to make contact with another person, to show identification, to mark status, and to decrease the possibility of threat (see Laver, 1975). The words *namaste* may simply mean "I bow to you," but when greetings are exchanged, people are also marking their cultural identity, cuing the degree of closeness or distance between one another, and decreasing the potential threat of a meeting. In short, greetings serve a number of important functions. Consider, for example, the beginning of this interaction between Gordon and Denise. These are two college students talking together on the phone. As you read the conversation, focus your energy on the beginning part of the conversation to see what the greetings might reveal about their relationship: Based on your reading, how intimate are these two participants? How close or distant are they? What is the nature of their relationship? What evidence is there in the talk to support your thoughts? (see Hopper & Drummond, 1992).

Denise:	Hello?
Gordon:	Denise?
Denise:	Yeah.
Gordon:	This is Gordon.
Denise:	Hi!
Gordon:	Hi, how are you.
Denise:	I'm okay, how you doin?
Gordon:	Alright, I have the cold now, uh I, I got a cold, I was at [Anita and Marc's place].
Denise:	Oh good huh huh huh.
Gordon:	Yeah really, did you enjoy your parents coming up here?
Denise:	They're, they've left already.
Gordon:	Oh really.

Let me unpack this moment with you. To begin, Denise picks up the phone. The utterance "hello" is a common way to answer the phone in the United States and it serves the important function of establishing the context for this relationship. In some countries such as France, for example, it is more appropriate to answer the phone with your last name. Gordon's next move is particularly interesting. Notice that after hearing her voice, he confirms that it is in fact Denise. She offers a token of agreement ("yeah") to confirm her identity and then he identifies himself.

Right away, then, Denise and Gordon are cuing that they do not know each other very well. When people know each other well, they can immediately recognize one another on the phone because a person's voice is a unique signature. So, when Denise answers with "hello," Gordon could have known right away that it was Denise and, thus could have continued the conversation in a different direction. Similarly, Denise could also identify him right away, but instead Gordon introduces himself. We have some cues, however, that they have some intimate knowledge about each other's lives. A few turns later, for example, Gordon asks, "Did you enjoy your parents coming up here?" In this question, Gordon shows some familiarity with something that is happening in Denise's life. The closer we are to the people in our lives, the more we know about what they are doing when they are not with us. In the next turn, in fact, Gordon shows that he did not know that her parents had left. The utterance "Oh really" functions as a way to show that this is new information for him. When looking at this interaction, then, we can see how Denise and Gordon are cuing the nature of their relationship. They have dated each other for a short amount of time: enough to know a bit about each other and not yet able to recognize each other's voice, or to be able to use terms of endearment such as "honey" or "my love."

Greetings, and the small talk that follows, serve important relational functions (see Coupland, 2000; Mirivel & Tracy, 2005). Researchers have shown that small talk is the way people at home and at work "do" being close and thereby "establish, maintain, and renew social relationships" (Holmes, 2000, p. 48). To illustrate this point, consider two examples that were recorded conversations in several organizations (Holmes, 2000, p. 49):

Example 1:
Context: Joan and Elizabeth pass on the stairs

E:	Hi Joan
J:	Hi, how are you
E:	oh busy busy busy
J:	mm terrible isn't it

Example 2:
Context: Jon and May pass on the stairs

J:	hello hello, haven't seen you for a while
M:	hi well I've been a bit busy
J:	must have lunch sometime
M:	yea good idea give me a ring

As seen in these excerpts, the greetings and subsequent small talk enable people to "do collegiality." These utterances serve "valuable bridging function, a means of transition to the main business of a workplace interaction…it warms people up socially, oils the interpersonal wheels and gets talk started on a positive note" (Holmes, 2000, p. 49). This is how people at work maintain their relationships.

Without greetings and small talk, it is impossible to create or maintain relationships. In one case, Holmes and her colleagues (see Holmes, 2003; Holmes & Stubbe, 2003) studied small talk between workers with intellectual disabilities and other employees. They realized that "while these workers are often highly skilled at the tasks they undertake in the workplace, those with intellectual disabilities often find managing social interaction in the workplace a major challenge" (Holmes & Fillary, 2000, p. 274). With this in mind, they sought to understand what was happening. To find answers, they started to record the interaction and analyze it closely. This moment is an example of what they found (see Holmes, 2003).

Context: Small talk between three workers at the start of the day. Heath is a worker with an intellectual disability.

Dan:	be a nice day when it all warms up a bit though
Rob:	yeah okay
Dan:	so you haven't done anything all week, eh you haven't done anything exciting, talk to any girls
Heath:	no
Dan:	oh that's all right then
Rob:	[laughs]
Dan:	you don't want to talk to girls, they're more, they're trouble Heath. They get you into trouble. Look at me. I would have been rich and good looking if I hadn't had girls. Now, I'm just good looking. See Heath
Heath:	no response

In this interaction, Heath's inability to do small talk is noticeable. He only provides a minimal response to Dan's question (i.e., "no") and then provides absolutely no response to Dan's joke. Holmes and her colleagues have found that workers with intellectual disabilities have a hard time managing social interaction and having good, friendly relationships at work. The source of the problem is that they do not know how to do small talk: Without it, they cannot sustain relationships at work. Without greetings and small talk, it is simply impossible to form and develop relationships. Our seemingly mundane and unimportant utterances thus serve the most important function of all: to create and maintain our social life.

The constitutive model of communication emphasizes that communication is not simply an exchange of information. As shown in this section, and according to Speech Act Theory, the utterances we use in everyday talk are speech acts that serve multiple, and often complex, functions. To draw on the positive communication model, our utterances can be used to greet, question, compliment, disclose, encourage, listen, or inspire. Our talk also helps us to create, discover, affect, or influence others. In the next section, I introduce conversation analysis and show that communication creates an immediate context for interaction.

Conversation Analysis

"If we can but realize that it is not how another acts that is of primary importance, but how each one of us acts and reacts, and that if reaction and action can be fundamentally, deeply understood, then relationship will undergo a deep and radical change."
—KRISHNAMURTI, 1992, P. 2

In the 1970s, a young sociologist named Harvey Sacks studied language in a completely new way. He recorded phone conversations, transcribed to put on paper what people said to one another, and began to analyze them closely to see what would emerge. In lectures at the University of California at Berkeley and Irvine, he brought short excerpts to his classes and spoke about them for the duration of class to discover the underlying mechanisms that gave structure to human conversation (Sacks, 1992). In one of his first lectures, delivered in 1964, Sacks introduced three examples of telephone conversations that were recorded at an emergency psychiatric hospital. These are the first two (p. 3):

Excerpt 1:

A: Hello.
B: Hello.

Excerpt 2:

A: This is Mr. Smith may I help you?
B: Yes, this is Mr. Brown.

In his lecture, Sacks unpacked some of his observations about these small bits of conversational data. A first observation is that a greeting most regularly takes place in two: a person says something (e.g., "Hello") and the other responds (e.g., "Hello"). Greetings, he showed, come in pairs. A second observation he made was that the nature of the first greeting shapes the next one. As he wrote: "If A says 'Hello,' then B tends to say 'Hello.' If A says 'This is

Mr. Smith may I help you,' B tends to say 'Yes, this is Mr. Brown'" (p. 4). The point here is that in choosing the form of the address, the first speaker can "thereby choose the form of address the other uses" (p. 4). Sacks's analysis was the birth of Conversation Analysis. In this section, I introduce Conversation Analysis and several of its concepts.

Conversation Analysis (often referred to as CA) is the study of talk-in-interaction. It emerged from the work of Harvey Sacks and his colleague Emanuel Schegloff (1968). CA is both a method for studying human conversations as well as a theory through which to understand social interaction. As a theory, CA has three main features (Mandelbaum, 2008). First, CA suggests that talk is an action. In this regard, it echoes Speech Act Theory and sees all utterances as actions that are performing one or more functions. Second, CA proposes that all actions in everyday talk are deeply structured. That is, there are organizing principles and mechanisms that speakers use, or adhere to, to "make" conversation in everyday talk. Finally, all actions that speakers produce are locally organized. That is, communication is meaningful in light of what participants are doing in the moment of action: a person speaks and another responds. To illustrate CA's guiding principles, I focus here on the concept of adjacency pairs and the related concepts of utterances as context-shaped and context-renewing.

One of the most groundbreaking ideas from Harvey Sacks is his discovery that conversations are organized and structured around **adjacency pairs**. Conversations involve speech acts that are produced in a particular sequence. One person says something and another person responds. Last night, for example, I put my son Hugo to bed and this interaction took place:

Papa:	(speaking softly) I want to tell you something Hugo (I lean into him, close to his ears). You are an amazing kid.
Hugo:	(softly in my ear) I want to tell you something Papa. You're the best dad.

In this moment, a father and a son are speaking to each other. I am complimenting him and he is responding to it by also issuing a compliment. Note that the conversation feels complete in part because both persons are making a move, with one move completing the previous move. Said differently, the conversation makes sense because it has two utterances that complete each other. This is exactly what Harvey Sacks (1992) noted in his studies of conversation: Conversations are organized by pairs of speech acts that typically come together. A greeting, for example, typically implies another greeting.

An offer typically makes possible an acceptance of that offer or a refusal. Or in the case of Papa and Hugo, a compliment may invoke a compliment. With the concept of adjacency pairs in mind, utterances can be seen as either being a first pair part or a second pair part. Sometimes, as we saw in the example above, the pairs of speech acts are adjacent to one another: the second pair part occurs immediately after the first pair part. But this is not always the case. Here is a brief example of a conversation between two lovers:

Corinne:	Tell me something true.
Christian:	(hesitating) (pausing) Are you sure you want to know?
Corinne:	Yes
Christian:	I think I'm in love with you.

In this interaction, notice that Corinne makes a request with a question of sorts: "Tell me something true." The next utterance, however, is not the response to Corinne's request. Christian is asking a question. Corinne, in turn, provides a short answer to that question: "Yes." Then, in the fourth turn, Christian finally provides the answer to Corinne's original request. Therefore, there are in fact two adjacency pairs that are organized in this way:

Corinne:	First Pair Part 1
Christian:	First Pair Part 2
Corinne:	Second Pair Part 2
Christian:	Second Pair Part 1

The concept of adjacency pairs is fascinating because of its implications. One implication is that all conversations are organized and structured around a basic structure of two speech acts or utterances. The more important implication is that every utterance that is spoken *implicates a particular course of action*: a first pair part is an action that inherently creates a reaction. A person's conversational turn, thus, will have the implication of setting in motion a localized context under which the other person must operate. Said simply, what you say affects what the next utterance will be. The next person's move will then have the same power of influence: constraining or liberating the talk, narrowing the focus of the conversation, and putting the other person in a context of possible responses. For example, Corinne's utterance "Tell me something true" opens the floor for a variety of responses. Her request for information does not suggest what the answer is, but by asking the question in this way, she is implicating Christian in a specific course of action: to make a statement that is true. Every person is free to choose to answer a question or not, to make a statement or not, and to do so amid an almost infinite amount of possibilities—that is why the act of communicating can be seen as an act of creativity and why sometimes the spoken word verges on poetry. A person can simply create an infinite amount of utterances. However, the demands of a move are such that a person's piece of talk will often exercise an interactional momentum—the first pair part will naturally place the next utterance in a context of responses.

The concept of adjacency pair illustrates well the constitutive view of communication. As seen above, conversations are constructed speech act by speech act. Each utterance has an immediate, pressing impact on the next utterance. Moment-by-moment, turn-of-talk by turn-of-talk, people are co-creating the unique social reality that they are experiencing because their moves are uniquely organized around the choices that they are making in an immediate context of possibilities. Each conversation is thereby inherently unique and irreproducible because each person is producing an action in real time out of thousands of possibilities.

Every speech act is thus responsive to a previous context and shaping the next one. As conversation analysts have long argued (see Drew & Heritage, 1992; Heritage, 1984) our "utterances are doubly contextual" (p. 18); an utterance is both **context-shaped** and **context-renewing**. An utterance is context-shaped because it reflects a larger environment in which it takes place and is typically responsive to an immediate activity, including a person's talk. As we saw above, Christian's answer is meaningful in part because it responds to Corinne's request; it is thus immediately responsive to the context that she has set in motion. But there are also other contexts that are shaping his utterance: the nature of their relationship, how intimate they are, how long they have seen each other, where they are located, what culture that they are a part of, as well as all of their previous experiences. All of these elements form a context that people draw on in a way that also shapes what utterance will be spoken.

The fact that an utterance is context-shaped is easily understood because it makes intuitive sense. We know that the context surrounding the way we speak is affecting what is actually being said. Our utterances, however, also are context-renewing. Each utterance that is spoken brings to life a context for interaction. It is creating and bringing forth the reality under which people will operate. As Drew and Heritage (1992) explained, "the interactional context is continually being developed with each successive action" (p. 18). Viewed from this perspective, people's roles, identities, relationships, or the institution they are a part of is enacted in the course of human interaction.

Since every utterance is context-shaped and context-renewing, every utterance is a turning point in the co-construction of social worlds. Consider Figures 2.1 and 2.2 to illustrate this important point.

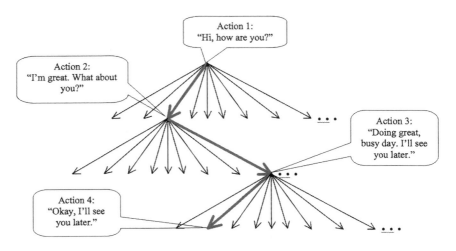

Figure 2.1. An Utterance Shapes the Next One.

As seen in Figure 2.1, an utterance inherently implicates a next relevant action. For example, as seen in this diagram, if you greet another person with "Hi, how are you?," you invite the other person to respond to a greeting. Notice, however, that there are many ways of greeting someone. You can say "What's up, dude?," "What's down?," "Hi, Dr. Jones," or "Good morning, my love." Each of these options can create an entirely different course of action and shape what the other person will say. The next person, however, also has many choices, but these choices are related to the prior course of action. If the other person responds with "I'm great, what about you?" she has chosen only one option amid countless possibilities. Through her utterance, she too sets in motion what happens next. This process is going on at all times, moment-by-moment and turn-of-talk by turn-of-talk. Every utterance, thus, is a response to a previous utterance and shaping the next one. This means that people co-create their interaction one utterance at a time. One difference in a person's move and the interaction could move in a completely different direction. Every interaction is thus inherently dynamic.

In Figure 2.2, consider how the difference in the response from the second person affects the subsequent turns of talk.

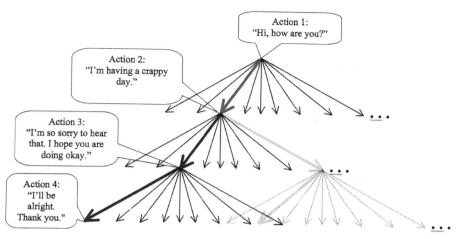

Figure 2.2. A Change in One Utterance Changes the Whole Conversation.

The first utterance is the same as in the first diagram. The first speaker says: "Hi, how are you?" This act, as we saw, sets in motion a course of action about what to say next; it influences what will be said. But, the next speaker chooses a different response. Rather than answering positively, the person complains: "I'm having a crappy day." By choosing a distinct course of action, these two communicators are now constructing an entirely different conversation. In fact, the second action has a strong impact on how the rest of the conversation unfolds. *Our utterances, therefore, affect what comes next.* What you choose to say makes a difference.

In this section, I introduced Conversation Analysis. First, I explained the concept of adjacency pairs to show that our conversations are created in pairs of talk: a person says something and the other person responds. Second, I focused on the idea that utterances are context-shaped and context-renewing. Together, these concepts illustrate that an utterance creates an immediate context for interaction and that people co-create unique communicative moments. With this knowledge in mind, the next section focuses on practice.

Practical Knowledge

In the Disney movie *Pocahontas*, there is a scene among Grandmother Willow, a tree wiser than time, Pocahontas, and her beloved John Smith. In the scene, Grandmother Willow gathers them together and speaks:

Grandmother Willow:	Now then, there's something I want to show you. Look. [dips her vine in the water in which glowing ripples begin to form]
Pocahontas:	The ripples.
John Smith:	What about them?
Grandmother Willow:	So small at first, then look how they grow. But someone has to start them.

In the first part of the chapter, I proposed that positive communication creates contact. I supported this principle by introducing the constitutive view of communication and two major theories of communication: Speech Act Theory and Conversation Analysis. Together, these theories emphasize that an utterance is an action that affects the next utterance. This is particularly true of the act of greeting others, which often serves the function of acknowledging the presence of another person and making contact. In this part of the chapter, I focus on the practice of greetings. First, I explain that the act of greeting is an important example of positive communication. Then, I invite you to reflect on your greeting practices, to study greetings, and to practice greeting others.

Greeting as Positive Communication

The act of greeting is an example of positive communication. As illustrated above, greetings serve crucial functions in processes of human interaction. Greetings often function as a way to appease potential aggression (Firth, 1972), acknowledge the presence of others (Searle, 1969), begin interaction, and set in motion what is going to come next in the interaction (Schegloff, 1968). Greetings are a crucial part of all relationships, at work or at home.

There is substantial research across fields of study that supports the idea that greetings are consequential. Researchers, for example, know that the presence or absence of greetings matter greatly in long-term relationships. Research on couples who have been married more than 50 years cite greetings as one of five most important behaviors in their relationship (see Young, 2004). In the workplace, Waldvogel (2007) found that greetings affected the entire culture of an organization. After comparing two organizations, one with a harmonious climate with open and positive relationships and another with low staff morale and mistrust of management, the author found that in the company with a strong positive culture, employees consistently used greetings and closings in their email exchanges; in the other organization, most people focused on the information only. In education, researchers have found that students who are greeted by their teachers perform more effectively on examinations and that it affects their learning (e.g., Berstein-Yamashiro, 2004). In addition to research on greetings, we know instinctively in our own lives that being greeted can be memorable and that it can carry positive consequences. In short, the act of greeting serves positive functions in a variety of contexts and is a universal practice. As Duranti (1997) wrote, "greetings are an important part of the communicative competence necessary for being a member of any speech community" (p. 63). It is a speech act that is worth reflecting on, experimenting with, and practicing.

Reflect on Greetings. Greetings are a natural part of every person's interactional life. Every person has natural tendencies in terms of what situations make them comfortable to initiate contact with others and what situations may create a tendency to withdraw or avoid greeting others. As a reflection exercise, spend the next five days observing your own behavior in action. Pay attention to the openings of conversations as well as your tendencies to initiate greetings or to avoid making contact. The purpose of the activity is to simply become more aware of your behavior as it relates to conversational openings and greeting sequences. In your observations, consider these questions:

1. How often do I greet?
2. Whom do I greet? Whom do I not greet?
3. When do I initiate greetings? When do I wait to be greeted?
4. How authentic are my greetings? When am I most authentic or least authentic?
5. When is it easy for me to greet? When is it most challenging for me to initiate a greeting?
6. What tensions or challenges do I face in the openings of conversations?
7. What are my tendencies? What are my preferences?
8. What impact(s) do my greetings seem to have on others?
9. What do I experience when others greet me? What is a typical response from me?
10. What are my strengths? What are my weaknesses?

These 10 questions provide a starting point. At the end of each day, write down your main observations. Remember that the objective is simply to become aware of your communicative patterns, not to judge or evaluate those tendencies. After five days of observations, write down the three things that you have learned about your communication style.

Study Greetings. Conducting research is an important way through which to learn about greetings. The purpose of this small research experiment is to understand whether, and how, greetings can be memorable in a person's life. Your objective is to interview four strangers. Each interview should last about 10 minutes. To guide this small research project, use the following interview schedule:

Introduction

Hi! My name is _____. I am a communication student at the university. I'm doing a short research study to understand whether, and how, greetings can be memorable in a person's life. I would like to interview you for about 10 minutes to find examples of memorable greetings in your life. If you agree to be interviewed, I will ask you five questions about a greeting that is memorable to you. Feel free to answer the questions to the best of your ability. [After gaining consent, you can begin the interview.]

Questions:

1. Tell me about a time that someone greeted you that is memorable to you.
2. What happened during this moment of communication?
3. How has this moment affected you?
4. What consequences has the greeting had on your life?
5. How has this moment influenced you?

Conclusion

Thank you so much for participating in this short interview. I really appreciate your help. I hope you have a great day. Thank you again.

After conducting the interview, reflect on the major finding from your study and what story best exemplifies the impact that greetings can have on others. Then, share this story with at least one person.

Practice Greetings. Initiating greetings or making contact with others is a choice. It is a decision people make based on the values that drive them. Often, it is an act of courage. But, given how influential greetings can be, it also is a skill that can be practiced at home and at work. Good communicators can learn to reach others and connect. The purpose of this practice session is to expand your ability to greet others across different cultures. It is obviously difficult to master multiple languages, but all it takes to make contact is one utterance. Thus, this practice invites you to learn how to greet in multiple languages. Greeting others in a person's native language establishes a good foundation for contact, shows intercultural sensitivity, and sets in motion a positive relationship. These are 10 ways to greet others in different languages.

In French:	Bonjour
In Malay-Indonesian:	Selamat pagi
In Portuguese:	Bom Dia
In Bangali:	Ei Je
In Arabic:	Al salaam a'alaykum
In Russian:	Zdravstvuite
In Spanish:	Hola
In Hindustani:	Namaste
In Chinese:	Ni hao
In German:	Guten tag

Being able to initiate greetings in different languages gives a person more alternatives for beginning a conversation. When it is done, it can set in motion a unique context for interaction and bridge cultural differences.

Summary

This chapter has shown that positive communication creates contact and that greetings are a fundamental example of positive communication. To support these ideas, I introduced the constitutive model of communication, which suggests that social realities are created by human interaction. Then, I described Speech Act Theory and Conversation Analysis to show that utterances serve functions and that an utterance creates an immediate context for interaction. With these theories in mind, the second part of the chapter introduced the act of greeting as an example of positive communication to practice. Greetings, I showed, serve important relational functions and cultivate our ability to connect with others. Greeting is one important way of making contact: it connects people momentarily, but it also sets in motion the potentiality of great love or great friendship. One greeting is all it takes to make contact.

Further Reading

Austin, J. L. (1962). *How to do things with words*. Cambridge, MA: Harvard University Press.
Coupland, J. (Ed.). (2000). *Small talk*. New York: Longman.

Craig, R. T. (1999). Communication theory as a field. *Communication Theory*, 9, 119–161.

Csikszentmihalyi, M. (1990). *Flow: The psychology of optimal experience*. New York: Harper Collins.

Krishnamurti, J. (1992). *On relationship*. New York: Harper Collins.

Sacks, H. (1992). *Lectures on conversation* (2nd vol.; G. Jefferson, Ed.). Cambridge, MA: Blackwell.

Satir, V. (1976). *Making contact*. Ann Arbor MI: University of Michigan Press.

Youssouf, I. A., Grimshaw, A. D., & Bird, C. S. (1976). Greetings in the desert. *American Ethnologist*, 3(4), 797–824.

Key Conceptual and Theoretical Terms

transmission model of communication

constitutive view of communication

utterance

semantic, syntactic, and pragmatic meaning

speech act

Speech Act Theory

Conversation Analysis

adjacency pairs

context-shaped and context-renewing

· 3 ·

POSITIVE COMMUNICATION DISCOVERS THE UNKNOWN

Prelude

In Paulo Coelho's (1993) book *The Alchemist,* an old man tells Santiago, the main character in the fable, the following: "When you want something, all the universe conspires in helping you to achieve it" (p. 22). Perhaps there is energy in the universe that moves each of us in the direction of our growth, our potential, our dream. In his work, Maslow (1968) explained that "people are both actuality and potentiality" (p. 41). Between actuality and potentiality stands growth. Maslow wrote:

> We fear our highest possibilities (as well as our lowest ones). We are generally afraid to become that which we can glimpse in our most perfect moments, under the most perfect conditions, under conditions of greatest courage. We enjoy and even thrill to the godlike possibilities we see in ourselves in such peak moments. And yet we simultaneously shiver with weakness, awe, and fear. (p. 34)

Moving in the direction of our dreams is not easy, but I have found a practice that helps me. First, I articulate precisely in my mind what I want. Then, I ask the universe for it politely, with great respect, and disseminate my energy in the cosmos by speaking it aloud. Try it like this:

Dear Universe,

I know that you are very busy. This may be too much to ask, but I would really love it if I could [fill in the blank]. Thank you so much for considering this request. I promise to return the favor by giving you M&Ms (I have found that the universe really likes M&Ms).

Once you have asked the universe for what you want, then just get to work. Use the energy in the cosmos to accomplish your dreams, and throw a few M&Ms in the wild to return the favor.

Introduction

"This is my daughter the other day. She's like, 'Papa, why can't we go outside?' 'Well, cause it's raining.' 'Why?' 'Well, water is coming out of the sky.' 'Why?' 'Because it was in a cloud.' 'Why?' 'Well, clouds form when there is vapor.' 'Why?' 'I don't know. I don't know any more things. Those are all the things I know.' 'Why?' 'Cause I'm stupid okay.' 'Why?' 'Well, because I didn't pay attention in school, okay? I went to school, but I didn't listen.' 'Why?' 'Cause I was high all the time. I smoked too much pot.' 'Why?' 'Cause my parents gave me no guidance.' 'Why?' … I'm going to stop here to be polite to you for a second, but this goes on for hours and hours and it gets so weird and abstract. At the end, it's like: 'Why?' 'Well, because some things are and some things are not.' 'Why?' 'Well, because things that are not can't be.' 'Why?' 'Because then nothing would not be. You can't have nothing isn't. Everything is. okay?'"

—LOUIS C.K.

Everyday conversations involve asking questions and giving answers. All relationships depend on this structure quite significantly. Think of the questions we ask: How was your day? Where should we eat? Did you see my keys? What do you want to do this weekend? Question-answer, question-answer, question-answer: that's how relationships operate. This point was well noted by Harvey Sacks (1992), who wrote: "there looks to be a rule that a person who asks a question has a right to talk again afterwards. And that rule can provide a simple way of generating enormous masses of sequences of talk: Question, talk, question, talk, etc., etc." (p. 49). Questions and answers are an intrinsic part of all relationships.

In this chapter, the focus is on the way we ask questions. I introduce the second principle of the Model of Positive Communication and its related behavior. The principle states that positive communication discovers the unknown. The first part of the chapter provides the theoretical background to support this principle. In the section, I introduce Coordinated Management of Meaning theory and the conceptual distinction between open-ended questions and closed-ended questions. The second part of the chapter focuses on increasing your practical knowledge by asking open-ended questions in everyday life. I end by describing a reflection exercise, a small study you can conduct, and a way to practice open-ended questions.

Theoretical Knowledge

This chapter is grounded in the principles of Coordinated Management of Meaning Theory. The theory emerged in the 1980s (see Pearce, Harris, & Cronen, 1981) and has become one of the most influential theories in the field of communication. One reason it is so influential is that the theory reminds professionals and everyday communicators alike that the choices they make in communication are consequential. In this section, I introduce the theory, its principles, and a few selected concepts. With this theory as a background, I explore how questions are used in human interaction. I focus on three contexts: medicine, news interviews, and personal relationships. Through analysis, I show how changing the form of a question can co-construct better social worlds.

Coordinated Management of Meaning Theory

In spring 2011, a student enrolled in my interpersonal communication course enters my office. He says: "I need to talk to you." He begins by describing the situation that he is in. He says he is not doing well: he is experiencing profound sadness. He lost two of his friends to suicide. He describes some of the events, including the words that were exchanged: "You're worthless. You might as well kill yourself," someone said during a conflict. The other person listened. Then, he keeps talking: "Everyone around me is in a coma. They think that they understand, but they don't. What we talk about in class is real, but no one is really seeing it." He keeps going, but I have a hard time following. So, I ask: "Okay, if you had to explain in one sentence what it is that you've realized, what would you say?" He pauses. He looks down. He makes eye contact again and speaks from his core: "Life is too short to live without love or with regret."

Communication is consequential. The spoken word affects people: who they are and who they can become. Often, the consequences are unanticipated or not thought about, in part because we can't always predict what our utterances will do. The act of speaking carries consequences because it has effects beyond itself that are both controllable and uncontrollable, intentional or unintentional, conscious or unconscious. The consequences can be both positive or negative. Our words can create hope, affect another person to take action, improve a relationship, or damage it. The consequences can be small or large, influential or minimal. But our communication has meaning beyond itself. One theory that highlights the consequentiality of communication is the Coordinated Management of Meaning Theory (henceforth CMM), which was developed by W. Barnett Pearce and his colleagues (see Pearce, 1989, 1994; Pearce & Cronen, 1980; Pearce & Pearce, 2000a, 2000b). This section introduces CMM and some of its core ideas.

The **Coordinated Management of Meaning Theory** (CMM) is a practical theory of human communication. It emphasizes some principles about communication that align with Speech Act Theory and Conversation Analysis. Much like Speech Act Theory, for example, it treats communication, including all talk, as a form of action (see Pearce & Pearce, 2000a). Second, CMM is similar to Conversation Analysis in that it sees that people in interaction are co-constructing their social worlds at every moment of talk: speech act by speech act, utterance by utterance, moment by moment. However, CMM does more than describe how communication works and offers a framework for improving the practice of communication.

First, CMM suggests that people in conversations are creating a particular kind of social world. Communication is the primary social process through which social and interactional realities are brought to life. As Pearce and Pearce (2000a) explained, CMM is "grounded in the belief that what persons-in-conversation actually say and do in relation to each other is the 'stuff' that makes what otherwise might seem dominating realities such as class, gender, ideology, and personality" (p. 408). Practically, this means that communicators can create conversations that may not exist without purpose and can shape the development of relationships in a productive direction.

Second, CMM "envisions persons as engaging in proactive and reactive actions intended to call into being conjoint performances of patterns of communication that they want and precluding the performance of that which they dislike or fear" (Pearce & Pearce, 2000a, p. 410). This process is called **coordination**. That is, according to CMM, persons-in-conversations can choose how to communicate and therefore can co-construct better social worlds together. Communicators can ask themselves, "What are we co-constructing together?" (p. 410) and find new ways to relate. From the perspective of CMM, "The

Think about what you

form of communication, fully as much as the context of what we say, or destroys our personalities, relationships, and institutions" (p. 413). People, thus, can learn to engage in forms of communication that cultivate the self, their relationships with others, the communities of which they are a part, and the society in which they live.

To engage in forms of communication that create better social worlds, CMM proposes that each act of communication is located "simultaneously within a series of embedded contexts of stories about persons, relationships, episodes, and within an unfinished sequence of co-constructed actions" (Pearce & Pearce, 2000a, p. 410). First, this means that the meaning of an act of communication is first shaped by complex layers of influences: the relationship between the people, the culture that participants are a part of, the identities and personalities of the persons-in-conversations, as well as the overall episode of which they are a part. **Episodes** are "thought of as bounded sequences of acts, with a beginning, middle, and an end" (p. 414). A job interview, a family dinner, and a school board meeting are all examples of episodes. Second, the point is that an act of communication responds to previous act(s) as well as sets in motion the next act(s). As Pearce (2007) explained, every act of communication has an **afterlife** "in the memories of those involved and in the experience of those affected by it" (p. 2). An act of communication thus serves functions in the present, but also serves functions in the future. Our speech acts have an effect beyond the present moment.

From the perspective of CMM, the speech acts that people use matter because each act is participating in the construction of social reality. Asking questions is one kind of speech act that is particularly consequential. How we ask questions, their focus and form, can make a difference. A question can constrain or liberate, give freedom or control, convey information or discover another person more deeply. This point is the focus of the next section.

Forms of Questioning

Inside the word *question* is the word *quest*. Asking a question is one way of going on a quest and discovering the unknown. When we ask a question, we are placing ourselves in a position to discover, but some types of questions tend to foster the process of discovery more than others. All questions influence what the other person will say. Some questions constrain the next speaker's possibilities and give more or less freedom to what they can say.

Nature — open and closed questions

This difference is captured nicely by what researchers call **open-ended questions** and **closed-ended questions**.

By definition, closed-ended questions are "narrow in focus and restrict the other person's freedom" (Stewart & Cash, 2011, p. 57). Open-ended questions, however, are "expansive and allow respondents considerable freedom in determining the amount and kind of information to provide" (p. 56). In thinking about questions in this way, it is important to first understand that questions can be more or less open-ended or closed-ended. Think of it as a continuum: some questions are highly open, moderately open, neutral, moderately closed, or highly closed. In general, though, questions that are closed-ended tend to exercise more control over the other person and tend to focus on information gathering. Open-ended questions, however, tend to promote the discovery of another person and the nature of their experiences.

Closed-ended questions tend to constrain participants' answers. As an example, consider the interaction between an attorney and a witness during a trial for rape (Drew, 1992):

Attorney:	And during that entire evening Miss [James] it's your testimony that there was no indication as far as you could tell that the defendant had been drinking?
Witness:	No.
Attorney:	Now Miss, when you were interviewed by the police some times later, some time later that evening didn't you tell the police that the defendant had been drinking?
Witness:	No.
Attorney:	Didn't you tell them that?
Witness:	I told them there was a cooler in the car and I never opened it.
Attorney:	The answer uh may the balance be stricken your honor and the answer is no.
Judge:	The answer is no.

The pressures of answering questions at home versus in court are not identical, but questions nevertheless set in motion a particular course of action. Consider each question that the attorney is asking. In all three cases, the witness is asked to respond to the question in a particular direction: a "yes" or a "no." These are examples of highly closed-ended questions because they restrict the freedom that the person has in responding to the question and it calls on them to answer succinctly. A question is thus setting in motion the kinds of answers that are possible. It does not mean that the next person has no choice:

a person can always choose to answer however he or she likes. This is exactly what happens after the third question: the witness chooses not to answer with a "yes" or a "no" and instead provides additional information. People always can choose how to respond, but the question nevertheless provides a context for the next utterance. Notice, for instance, that the witness is not discussing how her day has been going, what her passion is about, or what she hopes for the future. The question is thus providing the kind of topic that is answerable or addressable.

Every question directs the other person's talk, affects what is revealed or not revealed, and can enable a person to express themselves or not. Closed-ended questions are valuable for controlling information, but they generally do not facilitate the process of discovery. In general, open-ended questions build rapport more effectively, provide others with freedom about how to answer, and are more personal and humane in character. Open-ended questions simply foster discovery and they tend to create deeper and more meaningful interactions. In the next section, I draw on communication research to show how important open-ended questions are in three major contexts. First, I draw on the research in health communication to show that open-ended questions function positively in meetings between physicians and patients. Then, I describe the use of questions in news interviews, showing along the way that open-ended questions promote discovery. In the third context, I focus on how questions are used in personal relationships.

Context 1: Questions in Medical Encounters. The use of questions is particularly significant when physicians communicate with patients. Across much of the research for the past 40 years on this topic, scholars have noted that physicians consistently have the tendency to ask closed-ended questions to control and monitor the interaction (see Thompson, Dorsey, Miller, & Parrott, 2003). Very often, in fact, physicians also use directives or commands to exhibit status and direct the flow of the conversation. Consider several examples of real interactions that were recorded by researchers.

Example 1 (simplified from Robinson, 2003, pp. 39–40)

Doctor:	Does that hurt right there?
Patient:	Mm, it doesn't, uhm, I can feel it, but it's not real painful.
Doctor:	and, right. Well, what I'm asking you is can I reproduce your pain by pushing?
	(several turns later)
	So again when I push on that tendon right there.
Patient:	yeah, I can feel that.

Doctor:	Yeah, I know, it's never pleasant, and I'm pretty good at smashing you know.
	But my question is, when I push on that is that much tender than this side?
Patient:	No.

In this example, note that the physician's first question. "Does that hurt right here?" is a highly closed-ended question because it implies a short response and begs the patient to respond with either a "yes" or a "no." Notice that the patient does not simply say "no" in part because our tendency as speakers is to provide a longer account when we do a refusal. Still, however, the response is minimal. The speaker does not expand and little is revealed about the patient's experience. In the next several turns, the physician asks questions that also are closed-ended: "Can I reproduce your pain by pushing?" and "When I push on that, is that much tender than this side?" Although these questions are perfectly legitimate and make sense given that the physician is seeking precise knowledge of the patient's experience, the research shows that physicians have the tendency to ask questions that mostly belong to this category of questions. One significant problem that has been documented is that closed-ended questions make it difficult to nurture relationships, build trust, and access more meaningful information. In the context of medicine, researchers have found that patients frequently have more than one concern to address, but because of the way that interaction unfolds, physicians do not get access to the most important information (see Platt & Gordon, 1999). Closed-ended questions feel efficient because of the time constraint that physicians have, but in the long term they pose the problem of not identifying patients' real concerns, needs, and problems. Consider another example.

Example 2 (simplified from Heath, 2002)

Patient:	Well I've had this sore throat on and off for weeks now
Doctor:	Oh, dear.
Patient:	And I've got a cough, but it's, it's, I feel as though I'm choking, you know, when I'm coughing, I'm getting
Doctor:	mm mh
Patient:	no relief from coughing, it's just sort of choking, it's sort of at the back of my throat
Doctor:	Do you bring any phlegm up when you cough?
Patient:	Well yesterday I managed to be sick and I did, you know, but normally it—
Doctor:	But you vomited then?

In this interaction, which was recorded for a study in a different country, we see a similar pattern. The patient begins by explaining the symptoms and the medical problem. When the physician begins the inquiries, he uses highly closed-ended questions to manage the interaction, limit the patients' turn of talk, and control the topic of the conversation.

Physicians naturally use closed-ended questions to guide their encounters with patients. These questions *feel* effective because physicians want to move quickly through the encounter, focus on patients' symptoms, and deliver a diagnosis with recommendations for treatment (see Robinson, 2003). But, illness is not just a physical phenomenon. There also is a psychological and social experience surrounding illness (Sharf & Vanderford, 2003). This is partially why physicians can conduct a stronger interview with patients by asking open-ended questions to understand the whole person. This point is well-illustrated by communication scholar Athena du Pré. In her study, du Pré (2002) shadowed a physician "who has found a way to do what some consider impossible—address patients' physical, social, and emotional concerns and do it without exceeding the average length of a biomedical visit" (p. 2). In the article, du Pré described six communication behaviors that this physician used to accomplish the impossible. For example, du Pré showed how this physician listened deeply to her patients, self-disclosed about her own experiences with illness, and expressed empathy. In addition, this physician conducted the interview by using many open-ended lifeworld questions. These are examples of questions that she asked in the course of her encounters. Consider how they contrast with the questions that you saw in the previous excerpts:

Doctor:	Tell me what's going on.
Doctor:	How is your husband? [or job, or children, or wife]
Doctor:	What else are you concerned about?

These three questions propose a different interactional context than the ones that we saw earlier. The utterance "Tell me what's going on" serves as a question and opens up the possibilities about what patients might reveal, gives freedom to the patient for determining what to disclose, and will naturally encourage patients "to bring up lifeworld concerns, even concerns they might be hesitant to broach without encouragement" (du Pré, 2002, p. 14). In each case, the questions foreground what researchers have called the **voice of the lifeworld** (see Mishler, 1984), or the way patients typically think and experience illness, but also the way illness might affect their everyday lives or how what is taking place in a person's life will affect the person's health. The question, "What else are you concerned about?" is particularly effective in this context first because it enables the physician to check for other medical concerns, but also because it opens up the possibility for patients to speak up about their experiences.

In this section, I showed that closed-ended questions have the tendency to narrow patients' answers, control the interaction, and limit the freedom that they have in responding. Open-ended questions, in contrast, tend to give voice to the patient and provide space for patients to describe their experiences with illness. As in the context of medicine, news interviewers often use closed-ended questions when open-ended questions would liberate the floor and foster a stronger relationship with the interviewee.

Context 2: The Use of Questions in News Interviews. Heritage (2003) explained that "questioning is central to the practice of news interviewing, and skill in question design is at the heart of the interviewer's craft" (p. 57). One of the core communicative challenges for interviewers is to be neutral while seeking the truth about issues and stances; this is why journalists often have to "design their questions to strike a balance between the journalistic norms of impartiality and adversarialness" (p. 59). This is difficult to do because how a person formulates a question will naturally reveal stances and attitudes toward issues. In this case, we can see again how closed-ended questions and open-ended questions will function differently.

To begin, let's consider an interview between George W. Bush and Carol Coleman, an interviewer from Radio Television Ireland. After the interview, the White House issued a ban on the video, refused to participate in further interviews with Carol Coleman who was scheduled to interview the First Lady, and complained about the lack of professionalism that Coleman displayed. Here are a few excerpts from the interview, including the opening from Carol Coleman:

Mrs. Coleman:	Mr. President, you're going to arrive in Ireland in about 24 hours' time, and no doubt you will be welcomed by our political leaders. Unfortunately, the majority of our public do not welcome your visit because they're angry over Iraq, they're angry over Abu Ghraib. Are you bothered by what Irish people think?
President Bush:	Listen, I hope the Irish people understand the great values of our country. And if they think that a few soldiers represents the entirety of America, they don't really understand America then.

...

Mrs. Coleman:	Mr. President, you are a man who has a great faith in God. I've heard you say many times that you strive to serve somebody greater than yourself.
President Bush:	Right.
Mrs. Coleman:	Do you believe that the hand of God is guiding you in this war on terror?
President Bush:	Listen, I think that God—that my relationship with God is a very personal relationship. And I turn to the good Lord for strength. And I turn to the good Lord for guidance. I turn to the good Lord for forgiveness.
	…
Mrs. Coleman:	You're going to meet Bertie Ahern when you arrive in Shannon Airport tomorrow. I guess he went out on a limb for you, presumably because of the great friendship between our two countries. Can you look him in the eye when you get there and say, it will be worth it, it will work out?
President Bush:	Absolutely. I wouldn't be doing this, I wouldn't have made the decisions I did if I didn't think the world would be better. Of course. I'm not going to put people in harm's way, our young, if I didn't think the world would be better….

These three excerpts illustrate well the tone of the conversation and how it was structured. The interaction does not end well and the relationship between the interviewer and the interviewee is strained. Although interviews are always co-constructed by the participants' talk, the interviewer has the power to set up the tone of the interaction and the kinds of answers that will take place. As Heritage (2003) has shown in his analyses of news interviews, an interviewer's questions will by definition establish particular agendas for interviewee responses. **Questions** set agendas by (a) "identifying a specific topical domain as the appropriate or relevant domain of responses" (p. 66), (b) "identify[ing] actions that the interviewee should perform in relation to the topical domain" (p. 67), and defining how narrow or broad the responses should be. In addition to setting agendas for the next turn responses, questions often "assert propositions and embody presuppositions with varying degrees of explicitness" (p. 71). Sometimes, questions are designed to set in motion the interviewer's preference about the kind of response that is expected. The point here is that asking a question shapes the next relevant turn of talk in a significant way. With this in mind, let's examine the questions that Carol Coleman is asking.

Her first turn of talk is the opening of the interview. The opening is crucial because interviewers can set up the tone, create a good relationship with the interviewee, and prepare for what is coming next to decrease uncertainty. Traditionally, this can be accomplished by first building rapport and providing information about the interview to decrease uncertainty. In her case, she sets up a problematic context immediately when she says: "the majority of our public do not welcome your visit because they're angry over Iraq, they're angry over Abu Ghraib." By starting the interview in this way, she is placing the president on the defensive and reflecting her position: she is revealing her stance on the issue and indirectly criticizing the president's actions. At the end of her turn, she asks a closed-ended question: "Are you bothered by what people think?" This question is a request for a "yes" or a "no" and thus narrows the president's freedom to talk. It also places him in a difficult situation since responding with "yes" would signal a negative emotion toward the public on his part and saying "no" would imply that he doesn't care about the public's perception. In addition, if he does not address the topic, he will be seen by the public as evading the question.

In the second excerpt, Carol Coleman is questioning the president about his faith. Notice how her utterance is forcing the president to talk about faith. In other words, she is establishing the topic of the conversation: the president, by structural sequence, must respond to her utterance. Then, she asks a closed-ended question again: "Do you believe that the hand of God is guiding you in this war on terror?" This question, much like in the earlier excerpt, narrows the president's options. If he says "yes," he can lose public credibility, but saying "no" would be dishonest and may place his faith in question.

The third excerpt exemplifies this pattern again. Mrs. Coleman sets up the question and affirms her stance. Then, she ends with a closed-ended question: "Can you look him in the eye when you get there and say, it will be worth it, it will work out?" This utterance proposes a short answer and implies either an agreement or a disagreement.

As these excerpts reveal, Carol Coleman consistently used closed-ended questions. The types of questions that she asked also are called "yes/no questions" because they place the interviewee in a position to respond with a "yes" or a "no." Interestingly, research has shown that "yes/no questions are recurrent sites of conflict" (Heritage, 2003, p. 67) between interviewers and interviewees. One main reason is that they control the interaction, place pressure on respondents to answer the question in a particular way, and narrow a person's options, and thus their conversational freedom. The interviewer's instinct is to ask closed-ended questions, but it creates a defensive environment, and actually prevents the possibility of good responses. Good interviewing is about discovery. Imagine how the interaction could unfold if Carol Coleman asked open-ended questions instead. For example, she could ask:

1. What are your reactions to the Irish people's stance against the war in Iraq?
2. How does your faith in God influence the decisions that you make?
3. What is the focus of your meeting with Bertie Ahern tomorrow?

These three questions are open-ended questions. They foster rapport, provide freedom for the interviewee to answer the question, and are designed to discover the person's perspective. Interviewing is first and foremost about relationship: maintaining a relationship with the interviewee and being able to reach a person's thoughts at a deep, fundamental level. Asking open-ended questions is a difficult communicative task but it can be done, even when interviewing a political figure. Consider this example in an interview with British Prime Minister Clement Attlee in 1951 (Heritage, 2003, p. 59; simplified):

IR: Good morning Mister Attlee, we hope you've had a good journey.
IE: Yes excellent.
IR: Can you—Now you're back hhh having cut short your lecture tour. Tell us something of how you view the election prospects?
IE: Oh we shall go in to give them a good fight. Very good, very good chance of winning, we shall go in confidently, we always do.
IR: And on what will labour take its stand?
IE: Well that we shall be announcing shortly.

In this interview, the interviewer consistently asks open-ended questions. The way the question is formulated is the strongest cue. The first question begins with "Tell us" and the second question starts with "What." Notice that in each case, the interviewer also does not project the interviewer's stance or position. When questions are designed in this way, they are called **neutral questions**. Neutral open-ended questions typically foster relationships more effectively. They focus on discovering a person rather than to control them, and give them freedom, which enables the interviewer to build trust and to promote self-disclosure. As Stewart and Cash (2011) explained, "open questions communicate interest and trust in the respondent's judgment" (p. 56). Closed questions, however, tend to control others and privilege the interviewer's goals. With these understandings, I now focus on how questions operate in intimate relationships to emphasize these principles. Questions fundamentally set in motion the nature of close relationships, and open-ended questions will foster more positive relationships.

Context 3: The Use of Questions in Personal and Social Relationships. As CMM suggests, our relationships with others are created by the way we interact with them. The way we ask questions of one another is thus fundamentally linked to what people co-create together. As we saw, questions will set in motion topics of conversations, influence the next person's talk, monitor the depth and personalness of a response, and enable the discovery of who a person really is and what they've experienced. Therefore, the questions that people ask in their personal relationships will naturally affect how people come to understand each other, how intimate they will be, and how much they will know about each other. If asking questions defines a relationship, then it is logical to assume that asking better questions will improve the quality of a relationship.

The use of questions is ubiquitous to personal relationships. Communicators can use both open-ended and closed-ended question in everyday talk. There is, however, a natural tendency for speakers to use closed-ended questions. Closed-ended questions are not necessarily always counterproductive, but they can become problematic, especially because they are used to control interaction and focus less on discovery than open-ended questions. In one study, Corbin (2003) examined a certain type of closed-ended question. She focused on the use of "did you" questions. She found that these types of questions were used frequently in personal relationships, but that they tend to foster relational problems. In her work, Corbin (2003) first showed that "did you" questions serve many functions in the course of interaction. Consider these three examples from her data.

Example 1: [Simplified, p. 163]

Student 1:   Hi Kim, did you get that tape from the Speech lab?
Student 2:   Yes, thank you so much for doing that.

Example 2: [Simplified, p. 163]

Husband: Did get the deal sold though.
Wife: Great.
Husband: So
Wife: Did you get your account straightened out?

Example 3: [Simplified, p. 163]

Mother:	Did you bring in the trash can?
Daughter:	Yes, I did.

In each case, one person is asking a "did you" question, but each question may serve a different function. For example, in example 1, the function of the question is to begin the conversation. In the second example, it is used to continue a "conversation when a previous topic has been talked about" (Corbin, 2003, p. 163). In the third example, the question is used "to remind someone of an intended action." In addition to seeing how "did you" questions serves several key functions, Corbin's study of these types of questions revealed that they often created interactional problems and were seen by people themselves as problematic questions. Often, in fact, the questions were followed by answers that placed the respondents in a position to account for their behavior, that is, to give "reasons for having done or not having done the action the question concerns" (p. 170). In the following conversation, Tom and Abbie are sharing dinner together (see p. 171):

Tom:	Have y— did ya do anything today for finance class?
Abbie:	For what?
Tom:	For finance class, did you get anything done?
Abbie:	No.
Tom:	Nothing at all.
Abbie:	Nada. I haven't done anything. I've been gone, since ten o'clock this morning.

In this conversation, Tom is asking several "did you" questions. In response, Abbie is showing that she is irritated with his questions. The question for us to think about is: Why? In this case, it is important to note that Abbie provides an account: "I haven't done anything. I've been gone, since ten o'clock this morning." When people provide an **account**, they do so because they have either broken a norm or an expectation, or they are accused of doing so, directly or indirectly (see Buttny, 1987). So, what's interesting here is that Abbie is interpreting Tom's question as a reproach. This is exactly what Corbin (2003) noted in her analyses: "The use of 'did you' at the beginning of the question indicates it is about a recipient's past action (or possible past action) and may be heard by the recipient to have problematic linguistic logical presuppositions" (p. 166). This point is well displayed in this short moment between two co-workers:

Pizza worker 1:	Did you grate this cheese?
Pizza worker 2:	What's wrong with it?
Pizza worker 1:	Well, you were supposed to put Saran wrap on it.

In this interaction, the first person asks a "did you" question. In response, the next person poses a question. His formulation of the question marks that the employee is taking the first utterance not as a question, but as an accusation. Interestingly, his interpretation is not inappropriate. The next utterance reveals that he has, in fact, not done something that is desirable.

Everyday communicators ask many questions: some of them are closed-ended and others are open-ended. When people are interested in getting to know another person deeply, the tendency is to ask open-ended questions. In one study, Cooper (2013) interviewed people to understand their **peak communication**. Peak communication is a term used to describe moments when people have communicated in a way that brought them a great sense of satisfaction, happiness, joy, or ecstasy. It also encompasses conversations that have been meaningful or impactful (see Gordon, 1985). One participant in her study shared an example of a conversation with his son. Here is how the interview unfolded:

EE:	The third little vignette was my own son. When we moved here to Arkansas in '74 or '75. Well, what age do kids start cotillion or dancing or whatever that is?
ER:	13 maybe?
EE:	Oh no, he wasn't that old.
ER:	Like fifth grade?
EE:	Yea, fourth or fifth grade. So, my wife felt that was important. They went through the process of applying. My wife is Caucasian and so my son is what we call half C or hybrid Eurasian. So, he got rejected. He didn't get accepted to go to cotillion which is so funny because they always need more boys than girls. He was denied because he was half Japanese. Which was sort of surprising, but I decided I better have a little chat with him. I said, *Do you know why you were not allowed to take part in cotillion?* He said yea, 'cause I'm half Japanese. I said, well, *What do you think about that?* He said, well you know, I like all my friends are doing it and they get to go out and eat pizza afterwards and, you know, I'd like to do it. He said, I kind of understand. I said, *What do you understand about it?* He said, you know, the people who were screening, were accepting students, had bad feelings about Japanese people. I said oh, well, *What do you think about that?* He said, well, and this is a great punch line, he said, you know, if I weren't half

Japanese I'd probably get to go. I said, yea. He said, but because I'm half Japanese you're my daddy.

This excerpt first illustrates the CMM principle that a few words can have a long-term impact on a person. Second, this short story illustrates how the father uses open-ended questions to discover his son's perspective. His son is being rejected on the basis of his race. The father could be outraged, share this outrage with his son, and criticize people, the school, and so forth. Instead, however, he approaches his son by trying to discover what he thinks about it: his perceptions, his thoughts, and the way that he makes sense of this event. Through this approach, he is thus able to capture his son's experience with the event without imposing his view. Notice the questions that he is asking:

1. Do you know why you were not allowed to take part in cotillion?
2. What do you think about that?
3. What do you understand about it?
4. What do you think about that?

With the exception of the first question, which could be framed in a more open-ended style, the interviewer asked three questions that gave voice to his son's perspective. In doing so, the conversation becomes more about how his son is making sense of the events affecting his life, than a lecture to his son about the injustice that he is facing. In the end, and through the use of open-ended questions, a father ends up connecting even more with his son.

In this section, I showed how questions are used in a variety of contexts, including medical encounters, news interviews, and everyday relationships. In each case, we have seen that closed-ended questions have the tendency to generate narrow responses that limit a person's talk. When a person uses open-ended questions, however, he or she is seeking to discover another person, to get to know them more deeply, to foster intimacy, and to give freedom to the other to reveal or not reveal. A question, as we saw, will inherently affect the next turn of talk. It sets in motion the parameters of the responses and the topic that can be addressed, but also creates the nature of the relationship that is at play. If questions and answers are at the heart of what relationships are about, then it is logical to assume that changing the way we ask questions will affect the nature of our relationships with others. With this position in mind, I now invite you to ask more open-ended questions in your life.

Practical Knowledge

Papa: Do you have any questions before you go to bed?
Hugo: Are you talking to me like a teacher?
          (both laugh)

The first part of the chapter focused on increasing your theoretical understanding of the importance and use of questions in human interaction. With CMM in mind, I suggested that changing the way you ask questions can change the nature of the relationships that you create. The principle that guides this statement is that positive communication discovers the unknown: it is used to discover a person more deeply and to reach mutual understanding. Now, the chapter focuses on practical knowledge: observing your tendencies in how you ask questions, conducting a short research project with open-ended questions, and to personally practice open-ended questions. First, however, I propose that asking questions exemplifies positive communication and is worth practicing in a number of social and professional roles.

Asking as Positive Communication

Asking good questions is not easy. It requires an interest in others, the willingness to discover, and a sense of curiosity. When a question is well-crafted, it can open up a relationship, discover new information, or change one's ways of thinking. Open-ended questions particularly serve positive functions. Closed-ended questions also can be productive and can, in fact, lead to open-ended questions (see Heritage, 2003). The point, thus, is not that closed-ended questions are always counterproductive or problematic, but that open-ended questions tend to move in the direction of discovery.

Communication researchers have long documented that how a person asks a question is consequential. In the context of health care, for example, researchers have shown that how patients ask questions have implications for their health and their adherence to treatment (Roter, 1984). Researchers also have shown that physicians' use of questions can affect the diagnosis, patients' health outcomes, and their adherence to treatment (Roter & McNeilis, 2003). In education, there is evidence that good teachers ask open-ended questions. In his study of the best college professors, Bain (2004) noted that "questions play an essential role in the process of learning and modifying mental models" (p. 31). Students "see the value of effective questioning for both increasing quality participation and for discussion effectiveness" (Dallimore, Hertenstein,

& Platt, 2004, p. 111). Open questions, Bain showed in his work, foster learning that is more effective. Open questions such as, Why are some people poor and other people rich? How does the brain work? What is the chemistry of life? illustrate how the great teachers start class. Whether it is at work or at home, asking questions simply matters. It is a speech act that is worth reflecting on, studying, and practicing.

Reflect on Asking. Asking questions is a natural part of everyday communication. As we saw in the chapter, many of our interactions are organized around this basic adjacency pair: question-answer. A person asks a question and an answer is delivered. Every person, however, develops certain patterns of behavior. We each have tendencies in the way we ask questions. The purpose of this observation exercise is to become more aware of your own tendencies when it comes to asking questions. For the next five days, observe yourself in action and consider these questions:

1. What kinds of questions do you ask at work?
2. What kinds of questions do you ask at home?
3. When you interact with children, what kinds of questions do you use?
4. When do you use open-ended questions?
5. When do you use closed-ended questions?
6. What are some missed opportunities in your everyday life for asking a question?
7. What questions do you wish you had the courage to ask the people who are close to you in your life?

These questions will enable you to reflect on your communication habits. After the five days of observation, write down three things that you learned about your own behavior. With this learning in mind, you can then conduct a small research experiment.

Study Asking. To explore the importance of open-ended questions, this research activity will ask you to explore people's experiences with peak communication. This exercise simply is one way to research this topic in your class. The purpose of the small research experiment is to capture three stories for each person that exemplify a moment of communication that brought a great sense of personal happiness, satisfaction, and joy. Your goal is to interview four individuals. Each interview should last about 10–15 minutes. To conduct your interviews, use the following interview schedule (adapted from Gordon, 1985).

Introduction

Each of us has memories of good conversations: moments of communication shared with others that brought a great sense of satisfaction, happiness, and fulfillment. In this interview, I would like to talk with you about peak communication that you have experienced at home or at work. My goal is to capture examples of peak communication in your life. Specifically, I will ask you to share three examples of peak communication.

Peak communication 1

1. Tell me about a first example of a peak communication moment for you.
2. How did this conversation take place?
3. What words do you remember being spoken?
4. What did you learn as a result of this conversation?
5. What were the long-term effects of this experience on your life?

Peak communication 2

1. Tell me about a second example of a peak communication moment for you.
2. How did this conversation take place?
3. What words do you remember being spoken?
4. What did you learn as a result of this conversation?
5. What were the long-term effects of this experience on your life?

Peak communication 3

1. Tell me about a third example of a peak communication moment for you.
2. How did this conversation take place?
3. What words do you remember being spoken?
4. What did you learn as a result of this conversation?
5. What were the long-term effects of this experience on your life?

Conclusion

Thank you so much for participating in this interview. I appreciate your stories and your courage for sharing them. Thank you again. Have a nice day.

Four interviews should give you 12 stories of peak communication. Use these stories to reflect about the importance of communication and how open-ended questions can help you discover others more deeply. Finally, identify your favorite story and share it with at least one person.

Practice Asking. Asking open-ended questions is a challenge. Based on my experience teaching interviewing and other communication courses, as well as my observations, my sense is that we all have a tendency to use closed-ended questions rather than open-ended questions. For students, particularly, it is often difficult to design open-ended questions. It requires creativity, an interest in others, and a change in behavior. There are many ways to practice asking open-ended questions. For this practice session, I share a repertoire of open-ended questions that you can use to discover the people around you. The purpose of the practice session is to ask open-ended questions to the people around you to discover them even more. You can also use these questions when meeting new people. By asking open-ended questions, you can discover others more deeply, create stronger bonds with them, and break down the appearance of difference. Practice these four questions.

1. What is your story?
2. What experiences in your life have shaped you?
3. What persons have affected your development and growth?
4. What conversations have made a difference in your life?

In asking these questions, we can seek to discover about one another and slowly realize that human beings, no matter where they come from, are much more similar than they are different. When you ask questions, you can discover.

Summary

In this chapter, I made visible that questions serve important functions in human communication. I argued that positive communication discovers the unknown. Put simply, the questions we ask help us discover others more or less deeply. This chapter first introduced CMM, a communication theory that proposes that people can co-create better social worlds through positive communication. Then, I explained the distinction between open-ended questions and closed-ended questions to argue that open-ended questions promote the discovery of others. Asking open-ended questions, I would say, is just one way of creating better social worlds. Specifically, I showed the value of using open-ended questions in three main contexts: in medicine, in news interviews, and in everyday relationships. In the second part of the chapter, I invited you to observe your own behaviors, to conduct a small research experiment on peak communication, and to practice asking open-ended question in your own life to cultivate more meaningful relationships. By asking open-ended questions, you can naturally discover the people around you with more depth, create a context for dialogue, and learn a great deal from the life experiences of others.

Further Reading

Coelho, P. (1993). *The alchemist*. (P. Coelho & A. R. Clarke, Trans.). New York: Harper Collins. (Original work published 1988).

du Pré, A. (2002). Accomplishing the impossible: Talking about body and soul and mind during a medical visit. *Health Communication, 14*(1), 1–21.

Heritage, J. C. (2003). Designing questions and setting agendas in the news interview. In P. J. Glenn, C. D. LeBaron, & J. Mandelbaum (Eds.), *Studies in language and social interaction: In honor of Robert Hopper* (pp. 57–90). Mahwah, NJ: Erlbaum.

Maslow, A. (1971). *The farther reaches of human nature*. New York: Penguin.

Pearce, W. B. (2007). *Making social worlds: A communication perspective*. Malden, MA: Blackwell.

Sacks, H. (1992). *Lectures on conversation* (2nd vol.; G. Jefferson, Ed.). Cambridge, MA: Blackwell.

Thompson, T. L., Dorsey, A. M., Miller, K. I., & Parrott, R. (Eds.). (2003). *Handbook of health communication*. Mahwah, NJ: Erlbaum.

Key Conceptual and Theoretical Terms

Coordinated Management of Meaning Theory
    coordination
    episodes
    afterlife
open-ended questions
closed-ended questions
voice of the lifeworld
questions
neutral questions
account
peak communication

· 4 ·

POSITIVE COMMUNICATION AFFECTS THE SELF

Prelude

I know that this has happened to you. You know what the right thing to do is: to tell your significant other how much you love him or her, to make a compliment to a colleague, or to greet your wife when she comes home. And yet, the voices inside of you are preventing you from doing it. You think to yourself: "Why should I initiate the greeting?" "Why isn't he taking care of me?" "What has she done for me lately?" When we communicate with others, we often have to manage the voices inside of us. This is why we can learn to quiet Self 1.

In his book, *The Inner Game of Tennis*, Gallwey (2008), a professional tennis coach who has worked with hundreds of players, noticed that learners of the game struggle to perform well because of a conflict between Self 1 and Self 2. Self 1, he argues, is the teller; it is the voice inside of us that comments negatively on our performance: it judges us, distracts us, and evaluates our behavior. Self 2 is the "doer," the part of us that performs the action. As Gallwey shows in his work, Self 2 is perfectly capable of performing without Self 1. The voices and commentaries about performance do not help tennis players perform better; neither do they help people who want to communicate better. As he explained, "This is the nub of the problem: Self 1 does not trust Self 2, even though it embodies all the potential you have developed up to that moment and is far more competent to control the muscle system than Self 1" (p. 11). In short, Self 1 often hinders the performance because Self 2 can perform well without the voices of judgment and evaluation.

People, Gallwey argued, perform better when they allow Self 2 to perform. To communicate well, thus, quiet Self 1; do not let Self 1 prevent you from doing what is best.

Introduction

"One has to tell a little child over and over again 'I love you,' but one 'I hate you' is all that is needed for a life-long negation of any further loving parental advances."

—HARRIS, 1967, P. 292

In *The Little Prince*, Antoine de Saint-Exupéry (2000) begins his story at the age of six. After seeing a picture in a book, he draws a picture of a boa constrictor that swallowed an elephant whole. He shows his drawing number 1 to the adults, but they can't find meaning in it. So, he makes a drawing number 2, but the adults still don't get it: "The grown-ups advised me to put away my drawings of boa constrictors, outside or inside, and apply myself instead to geography, history, arithmetic, and grammar. That is why I abandoned, at the age of six, a magnificent career as an artist" (p. 2). Fortunately, people can also influence one another positively.

In this chapter, I focus on how communication influences the development of the self. I foreground a third principle: positive communication affects who we are and who we become. Viewed from this perspective, every communicator is incredibly influential in the development and growth of others. The spoken word matters because it can be used to strengthen another. To proceed, the chapter begins by expanding your theoretical knowledge. In the second part of the chapter, I introduce the third positive communication behavior of the model, complimenting, and invite you to deepen your practical knowledge of communication.

Theoretical Knowledge

"It is not the case that humans exist and then enter into relations, but that as we relate and in our relating, our humanity is realized."

—STEWART, ZEDIKER, & BLACK, 2004, P. 28

Shared communicative moments with others are fundamental to our development. As Watts (1966) put it, "other people teach us who we are" (p. 70). To support this claim, I first introduce Symbolic Interactionism. Then, I focus on three major concepts. First, I introduce the concept of alter-casting (Tracy, 2002; Weinstein & Deutschberger, 1963). Second, I draw on the concept of ossification to explain how our self blends with the feedback from others (Blumstein, 2001). Then, I describe the work of the philosopher Mikhail Bakhtin (1984) and his concept of intertextuality. Together, these concepts and theoretical perspectives will illustrate that the spoken word has a tremendous influence on a person's development and growth.

Symbolic Interactionism

Although each of us might be born with certain personality traits, affinities, and interests, our interactions with others affect our sense of self, our identity, and the person that we become. A person's identity is constantly in the making through numerous interactions that we have with others. This idea is well-captured by a theory called **Symbolic Interactionism**, which is attributed to George Herbert Mead (1934). The theory is complex, but it essentially suggests that the "self ... is acquired as one is talked into membership in the human community" (Wood, 1994, p. 145; cited in Bergen, Suter, & Daas, 2006, p. 204). From a communication perspective, Symbolic Interactionism especially highlights two important principles. First, the theory argues that "communication is the primary way in which identity is negotiated" (p. 204), and second that "identity construction occurs through interaction with others" (p. 204). Together, these two tenets imply that interactions with others influence the development of the self.

From the perspective of symbolic interactionism, language is an important way through which meaning is negotiated and constructed. For example, the names used to refer to others help people co-construct various identities. "Mom" and "Dad" help to create parental identity; the use of "Doctor" can help cue the role of professor or medical professional; "honey" or "my love" can help to create closeness. Names are important for managing various identities, especially in family life.

In many families, for example, children refer to parents as "mother" and "father," or "dad" or "mom." Often, parents teach their children to use those names rather than first names as part of the socialization process. But, naming practices can be particularly challenging for some families. This point is well illustrated in a study by Bergen and her colleagues, who studied how lesbian co-mothers construct each other's identities as legitimate parents through the use of language. Specifically, Bergen et al. (2006) found that lesbian families use various address terms for the non-biological mother to create a parental identity. For example, the lesbian mothers who were interviewed often taught their child to use "mom" or "mommy" for both parents and did not allow the children to call them by their first name. This naming practice helped to construct both mothers as legitimate parents in the eyes of the child, in the eyes of the non-biological mother herself, as well as in eyes of others. As one person said in the interview:

> For me it's more of a validating thing. You know that if, if she were to call me Tina [I'd] feel kind of alienated you know from the whole mother thing...because I'm the non-birth mother, ah, it's just, it's just like she said, I wouldn't call my mom Cheryl, I call her mom because she's my mom and it's the same with Natalie...It makes me feel like I'm more of a real, permanent figure, family figure, mom figure in her life. (pp. 207–208)

Many mothers in the study echoed this sentiment. Being called "mom" or "mommy" constructed each person as a legitimate parent.

Symbolic Interactionism emphasizes that people's identities are both personally enacted and given to other people. Our sense of self, thus, is affected by the ways in which people interact with us. To echo the example above, a person is not simply a parent by thinking of himself or herself as a mother or father, but also by the way others act toward the person. The rest of this section focuses on this important point and describes three key concepts that illustrate the many ways communication affects the self. The first concept is called altercasting.

Altercasting

One concept that is helpful to think about the way identity is created through communication is altercasting (see Weinstein & Deutschberger, 1963). Defined simply, **altercasting** is the process by which we frame other people's identities or roles in our talk. The more complicated definition comes from Pratkanis and Gliner (2004), where they explain altercasting as "social interaction in which an ego (e.g., the source of a message) adopts certain lines of action (e.g., self descriptions, mannerisms, impression management, etc.) to place an alter (e.g., a message recipient) into a social role that specifies an interpersonal task (e.g., message acceptance or rejection)" (p. 281). In every utterance, we can cast others in certain roles, portray the way we think about them, or mark their identity in a particular way. This process is relatively complex and can take place obviously or with much more subtlety.

An obvious way of altercasting others is to assign an identity for the other person in the talk. As examples, consider these two excerpts, taken from a study of compliments in New Zealand (Holmes, 1986, p. 486).

Excerpt 1:
Context: the recipient's (R) old schoolfriend is visiting and comments on one of the children's manners.

Complimenter: What a polite child!
Recipient: Thank you. We do our best.

Excerpt 2:
Context: Mother commenting after a visit from her teenage daughter's new boyfriend.

Complimenter: Your new friend seems very nice dear.
Recipient: I'm glad you like him mum.

In both of these examples, the complimenter is assigning a positive characteristic to the speaker. In the first case, the first person is describing the other as a good parent. In the second, the complimenter is framing the recipient as someone who has good taste (Holmes, 1986). These compliments could be done even more explicitly (e.g., "you are a wonderful mother"), but they nevertheless assign to the recipient a characteristic that is positively valued. In her data, which involve more than 500 compliment exchanges, Holmes (1986) found that 65% of those exchanges expressed a positive affect. The top six positive descriptions included "*nice, good, lovely, beautiful, great, and neat*" (p. 490; italics original); those accounted for over two-thirds of all of the exchanges. This is how altercasting is done: we implicitly or explicitly communicate how we see others.

Altercasting is also more complex. It includes the subtle ways in which communicators give meaning to others. To see how this is at play, examine the following interaction in a reconstructed dialogue that had a long-lasting influence on a person's life.

Excerpt 3:

Renae:	So Kamesha I want you to know I consider you to be a strong team player and I just don't know what I would do without you.
Kamesha:	Thanks Renae. That means a lot especially coming from you. I certainly try my best and I truly enjoy working for you.
Renae:	The thing is I plan to retire in a few years and I know that you are in school. I don't see why you wouldn't be a perfect person to take over once I leave.
Kamesha:	Wow! I never thought about it but it does seem like a wonderful opportunity.
Renae:	So do you plan to go to graduate school?
Kamesha:	Well to be honest, I really want to go to law school. It's been my life long dream. I know it really doesn't tie in to this job but it's my dream.
Renae:	Don't be remorseful about following your dream. I think you can do whatever you put your mind to. You are smart and ambitious and I think you would be a great attorney. Good for you for setting your goals high.

In this interaction, Renae is Kamesha's boss. Notice how through her talk, Renae is giving meaning to who Kamesha is as a person. In the opening, Renae describes Kamesha as a "team player." Later, she emphasizes that she is "smart," "ambitious," and that she would be a "great attorney." These compliments can naturally affect Kamesha's sense of self, including her self-esteem. These utterances can be lenses through which Kamesha can see herself. In addition to this direct form of influence, Renae and Kamesha also are casting each other in specific roles. For example, they are both talking to one another as a boss and an employee: their power differential is being reflected in this conversation. Their roles are being produced by the way they interact and what they say to each other. Consider, for example, that the assessment "I consider you to be a strong team player" is making a compliment while simultaneously evaluating Kamesha as an employee. The label "team player" is one prototypical trait that employers see as desirable in employees. In the response, in fact, Kamesha responds to Renae as her supervisor. Her utterance, "I truly enjoy working *for* you," is one evidence that this is the case.

As the conversation proceeds, the roles shift to a mentor-mentee relationship. Once Kamesha discloses her long-term goal and marks that the offer for promotion is not her main interest, she is then placing Renae in a position to speak as a mentor rather than a supervisor. Her encouragements, "Don't be remorseful about following your dream" and "You can do whatever you put your mind to," are utterances in which she embodies that role. In the process of doing so, she thereby altercasts Kamesha as her mentee.

Altercating takes places consciously or unconsciously. Through talk, we frame our own identity and we place others in a particular role, too. These roles include being a friend, sister, father, son, supervisor, student, or secretary. Sometimes we know that we're doing it but much of the time our consciousness is not focused on trying to create the role we are embodying or creating the role of the other person. Yet, that's exactly what we're doing through our talk. One interesting implication of understanding the concept of altercasting is that the roles we take on are dependent on how we talk and how others talk to us. That is, our roles are *enacted* and *given* in the moment of human interaction. Our identities and roles, thus, are *not* fixed states of being: at any moment, we can act like a supervisor, mentor, friend, or brother. And other people, by altercasting us, can place us in that role, too. A second implication of the concept is that because our identities and roles are given to us, we depend on others to be and become a person. This is well-illustrated by the concept of ossification.

Ossification

The spoken word, if repeated enough, can influence a person's development. This claim is supported by Blumstein's (2001) concept of ossification. In his work, Blumstein drew on Symbolic Interactionism to describe the concept of **ossification**. As Blumstein argued, "if identities are projected frequently enough, they eventually produce modifications in the self" (p. 297). The concept of ossification is used to foreground the idea that people can influence each other. As he explained, "the process of ossification is very slow and gradual, and consequently is not easy to study with our conventional research methods. It is the process that we infer has occurred when we awaken one morning to discover we are not the same person we were twenty years earlier" (p. 297). Through interaction, Blumstein explained, people ossify each other in that they influence what each person is becoming. "If identities," he wrote, "are projected frequently enough, they eventually produce modifications in the self" (p. 297). One utterance at a time, we can thereby influence what another person is becoming. This idea is well-captured in this excerpt, both positively and negatively, in the autobiography by the tennis icon Andre Agassi (2009). We join a scene in which his father takes him out of a soccer field, tells him to put his tennis clothes on, and confronts him in the car.

> He shouts at the top of his lungs: You're a tennis player! You're going to be number one in the world! You're going to make lots of money. *That's the plan, and that's the end of it.*
>
> He's adamant, and desperate, because that was the plan for Rita, Philly, and Tami, but things never worked out. Rita rebelled. Tami stopped getting better. Philly didn't have the killer instinct. My father says this about Philly all the time. He says it to me, to mom, even to Philly—right to his face. Philly just shrugs, which seems to prove that Philly doesn't have the killer instinct.
>
> But my father says far worse things to Philly.
> You're a born loser, he says.
> You're right, Philly says in a sorrowful tone. I am a born loser. I was born to be a loser.
> You are! You feel sorry for your opponent! You don't care about being the best! …
> He says, You have a different mentality than Philly. You got all the talent, all the fire—and the luck. *You were born with a horseshoe up your ass.* (pp. 58–59)

In this narrative, Agassi describes well how a father's way of interacting with each child can influence the direction of his or her lives. Time and time again, Andre's father encourages him to see himself in a particular way: he has the killer instinct, he has the luck, he has the talent, he has the fire, and so forth. When Andre's behavior aligns with his father's perception, he pours it even more into him: you have the killer instinct, you have the talent, etc. Slowly and gradually, Andre's self-perceptions naturally align with the feedback from his father. A father's influence, after all, is tremendous. But this process can take place with anyone: our friends, our mentors, and perhaps also strangers.

The process of ossification is particularly visible in family interaction between parents and their children. The family is the locus of the socialization process, as children are taught particular sets of values, behaviors, and their sense of self in the process of interaction. These interactions can take place during family dinners (Blum-Kulka, 1997), on the way to school, or even during sports activities. For example, Kremer-Sadlik and Kim (2007) analyzed the recordings of everyday interaction in 32 families. They found that parent-child interaction before, during, or after sports activities played an important role in the socialization process. Consider this interaction that took place between a mother and her 10-year-old daughter Sonya.

Excerpt 4:

Mother: You guys won. What was the score? Two to one?
Sonya: Yeah
Mother: That was a good game. That's a close game.
Sonya: But did I do a good game?
Mother: You played a *great* game. You were well positioned. You had some *big* kicks.

In this moment, the mother uses an opportunity to compliment her daughter. She issues the compliment after her daughter requests an assessment of her performance, not just an assessment of the quality of the game. In this brief moment, the mother is contributing to Sonya's sense of self-worth. Interestingly, in a previous interview about Sonya, the mother had told the researchers that Sonya is not "assertive" and that playing soccer has given her more confidence over the last two years. The mother's compliment also participates in this process: the compliment is giving her confidence, too, particularly if it is done frequently. As the researchers explained, "by reinforcing her daughter's value for the team as well as her personal skills, Mother is contributing to her daughter's sense of self-worth" (p. 40).

Children can thus acquire their sense of self by the way parents interact with them. This is what ossification is all about. This principle is powerfully displayed in the novel and movie *The Help*. Aibileen, the main character, is a black maid in the 1960s serving a white family. While raising her 17th white child, Aibileen discovers a new way of thinking. Her idea emerges after consoling Mae Mobley, also known as Baby Girl, after a sharp criticism from her mother: "I told you to eat in your high chair, Mae Mobley. How I ended up with you when all my friends have angels I just do not know" (Stockett, 2009, p. 107). In response, Aibileen reaches for the child and speaks to her:

I touch her cheek. "You alright baby?"
She say, "Mae Mo bad."
The way she say it, like it's a fact, makes my insides hurt.
"Mae Mobley," I say cause I got a notion to try something. "You a smart girl?"
She just look at me, like she don't know.
"You a smart girl," I say again.

She say, "Mae Mo smart."
I say. "You a kind little girl?"
She just look at me. She two years old. She don't know what she is yet.

I say, "You a kind girl," and she nod, repeat it back to me. But before I can do another one, she get up and chase that poor dog around the yard and laugh and that's when I get to wondering, what would happen if I told her she something good, every day? (p. 107)

And so, she does. Every day, Aibileen talks to her: "I hold her tight, whisper, 'You a smart girl. You a kind girl, Mae Mobley. You hear me?' And I keep saying it till she repeat it back to me" (p. 107).

Ossification also is an important part of intimate relationships. As Blumstein (2001) explained:

A husband may learn for the first time that he cannot cook as his wife describes his culinary failures to a group of assembled friends. If he hears such commentary with sufficient frequency, both in front of guests and in solitary conversation with his wife, one may expect that he will come to incorporate culinary incompetence into his self. (p. 299)

Blumstein called this process, the way through which couples define one another through talk, as **couple identity work**. Interestingly, researchers have shown that the way couples define one another is consequential. For example, Sabourin and Stamp (1995) compared the talk of abusive and non-abusive couples during interviews and real interactions. They found important differences in their patterns of talk. One difference is that abusive couples tend to describe their experience with vague language (i.e., lack of detail and overall absence of events) while couples in non-abusive relationship use more precise language (i.e., marked by details and fullness in description). A second difference is that the talk of non-abusive couples was much more cooperative while abusive couples often were in opposition. A third difference was in the presence of criticisms, complaints, and compliments. Direct criticisms and complaints about the other person were frequent among abusive couples. Often, as exemplified in excerpt 5, these patterns emerged in the course of the interview.

Excerpt 5: (p. 233)

Wife:	If he's responsible and if he's in ... and if he's so good and if he's in control and he wants charge, looks to me like he could do something right, but he don't do nothing right as far as I'm concerned
Husband:	I just left the one out. Now that's all I left out is just the one.

Abusive couples often portrayed the other person negatively, and complaints and criticisms often were used even when it seemed unnecessary. On the other hand, non-abusive couples were more positive, talked with more optimism, expressed their emotional attachment, and peppered their talk with compliments. Excerpt 6 shows an example from the data.

Excerpt 6: (pp. 233–234)

| Husband: | I do understand what she has to do, what her day is like, and sometimes I wonder who has the hardest job ... The boys are very lucky to have someone like her. And I'm very lucky too. |
| Wife: | Well, my husband, he's an excellent provider. |

The use of compliments was particularly important to the relationship: it fostered the other person's sense of self, reaffirmed positive traits, softened a complaint if one was made, and created intimacy and closeness.

Every communication can weaken or strengthen another person, as well as the relationship that two people have. The concept of ossification illustrates that communication influences the development of a person over time: that the echo of certain utterances affect another. Criticisms and compliments can influence a person and the relationship in the long term. In the next section, I show how this is true in a real way by introducing the concepts of intertextuality and authoring.

Intertextuality and Authoring

"Two voices is the minimum for life, the minimum for existence."
—BAKHTIN, 1984, P. 181

What we say in our talk is often an echo of another person's voice. Although every person can be tremendously creative or poetic, many of our utterances do not belong to us; they are copies of already existing voices. The words "Good morning, how are you?" do not belong to anyone; neither does the phrase "an eye for an eye." Researchers in communication have now shown that our utterances often reflect the voices of others. In this section, I describe two concepts, intertextualization and authoring, to show that when we communicate, we influence the utterances of others, and thereby affect who they are.

Intertextualization is the process through which human beings' discourses blend together (Fairclough, 2003). The process of intertextuality is fairly complex, but there are some obvious examples. When children acquire language, they first learn to imitate and reproduce what they hear from the people around them. If a parent faces a young child and says "papa," the child will learn to imitate that utterance and produce it. Soon, the child will be able to say "papa." This is a basic example of two voices becoming intertextualized: a person says something and the other repeats it. When we learn a language, in fact, we learn to acquire words that do not belong to us; they are part of the language that exists independently of the individual. Language itself cannot teach anything: it is an abstract symbolic system. It is people who enact the language and thereby teach one another how to talk, what to say under certain circumstances, and what utterances are appropriate or inappropriate. As the philosopher Bakhtin (1986) wrote: "Our speech...is filled with others' words...[t]hose words of others carry with them their own expression, their own evaluative tone, which we assimilate, rework, and reaccentuate" (p. 89).

In the study of human interaction, researchers have long noted that one example of intertextualization takes place when people quote another person in their talk. This is called **reported speech**. As Wood and Kroger (2000) defined it, reported speech is "speech that is attributed by a current speaker to another speaker" (p. 103; also see Holt, 1996; Hutchby & Wooffitt, 1998; Tannen, 1989). Reported speech may be done directly or indirectly. **Direct reported speech** occurs when a speaker is quoting directly another person's words or their own. **Indirect reported speech** takes place when a speaker is paraphrasing another person's words or their own. These excerpts, taken from a study of bone marrow transplant survivors' online narratives, illustrate the difference (see Hamilton, 1998, p. 59).

Excerpt 7:

My doctor told me that I had almost no chance of surviving.

Excerpt 8:

The guy said, "Don't worry about it. See you in a year."

Excerpt 7 illustrates indirect reported speech because the words from the doctor are not directly reported. The second excerpt, however, shows direct reported speech in that the other person's words are quoted directly.

Reported speech serves many functions. Researchers have shown that people use reported speech to "make stories vivid and dramatic and to create involvement...as well as [serve as] a way of assigning responsibility for utterances to another person" (Wood & Kroger, 2000, p. 103). It can be used to strengthen one's point of view, undermine another, or can enable a speaker "to simultaneously convey his or her attitude towards the reported utterance"

(Holt & Clift, 2007, p. 7). Depending on the context, the speech being reported can be about someone who is absent or someone who is present. In this interaction, for example, direct reported speech is used. The conversation takes place at work in a meeting of three work colleagues in a government department.

Excerpt 9: (simplified from Holmes & Marra, 2004, p. 384)

A:	Let's go and talk to someone else. We'll get a completely different story about what to do.
S:	[Laughs]
A:	You know, the whole thing will just sort of grow into a soap opera.
V:	[Laughs] Yeah. This is, Christina came up with a good phrase before. I think we should adopt it in the office. She said "you need to account for the Len factor."
S:	The Len factor! I love it! Oh brilliant.
V:	[Laughs]
S:	I think Alex and I were talking about the Len factor yesterday. [Laughs] Oh yeah.
V:	Exactly. Thank you S; that's great.

This is a short moment between colleagues at work. The use of the term "Len factor" creates humor because Len is a colleague in the office who is known for delaying decision-making and progress by focusing on potential problems. The phrase, the "Len factor," was thus coined to "describe the unavoidable delay that must be built into an estimate of how long obtaining a response will take" (p. 384). Of importance, here, is the way in which the "Len factor" is brought to bear. In this moment, V uses direct reported speech by quoting directly what Christina said. For a brief moment, Christina's voice and V's voice are thus intertextualized. In this context, the function of the reported speech is to generate humor, create a sense of belonging for the team, while preparing the group for the planning process.

Sometimes, direct reported speech can be used with a person who is present. I found many examples of this practice when I observed group process therapy for six months with women recovering from addiction. During group therapy, the leading therapist often quoted directly from what patients were saying. Often, as is displayed in this example, the therapists used direct reported speech to raise the clients' consciousness and awareness about their own behaviors:

Excerpt 10:

Therapist:	Hold on, now hold on. Just like that, you switched, "so when I get upset, I get high." You stopped, you could almost touch it, it was so close to the surface … you can't well up yet and I respect that.

Sometimes, however, the direct or indirect reported speech was used to compliment clients' progress and to praise any significant change in behavior. This is well displayed in this therapist's comment:

Excerpt 11:

Therapist: Good job. You reframed it. You said, "I'll stay here with my family." You didn't pout. Good for you.... . I like the way you reframed that.

The reported speech occurs in the first line, when the therapist says, "I'll stay here with my family." Immediately, and following the quoted utterance, she highlights what the client did not do: "you didn't pout." Then, she offers a supportive remark: "Good for you." By drawing on the client's speech, the therapist is thus able to compliment a client's progress in the program and thereby encourage her to persevere.

Reported speech is a straightforward way of seeing intertextualization at play in human interaction. When reported speech takes place it is easy to see how a person's utterance is affecting the utterance of another person. Notably, however, most of our talk could reflect what we have heard or seen in writing, even though it is impossible to show in the course of our lives the extent to which a person's talk has affected the development of another, or how the combination of voices are working together to form our own. And yet, we imitate each other, repeat what we've heard, or paraphrase it in a more creative fashion. One truth about communication is this: our utterances can become part of the discourse of others.

The concept of intertextuality emphasizes that our voice is influenced by the voices of others. Our utterances reflect what we heard from others. In his work, Bakhtin (1990) pushed the idea further and explained that in this sense every person can become the *author* of another person. **Authoring** simply means giving a text to another person. Because utterances can be imitated and borrowed, we can influence one another's voice. Viewed this way, my voice has been intertextualized with everything that I have read and all of the persons with whom I have interacted. My speech has been authored by my father, mother, brother, friends, and mentors, as well as the students and strangers that I interact with.

In this section, I have introduced the concepts of intertextuality and authoring to show that what we say and do are reflections of others' voices. Viewed this way, a person's identity is a unique complex kaleidoscope of intertextualized voices authored by the myriad interactions a person has with others. Communication thus affects who a person is by providing a repertoire of utterances that can be drawn on. If every person can author the way we talk, this also means that every person can serve as a role model, including for how to handle a particular moment. Every interaction can be a moment of learning and can give each person increasingly more choices about what to say or do. In the next section, I move from the theoretical knowledge you have acquired to practicing positive communication.

Practical Knowledge

"Making real contact means that we make ourselves responsible for what comes out of us. Anything that injures self-esteem reduces the opportunity to make good contact."
—VIRGINIA SATIR, 1976

In the first part of the chapter, I introduced Symbolic Interactionism and several key concepts to support the principle that positive communication affects the self. Together, these ideas illustrate that each person affects others' sense of self. With this theoretical knowledge, each person can choose to affect others positively or negatively. The second part of the chapter draws on this theoretical understanding to practice communication more positively.

In his work on self-actualization, Maslow (1968) argued that **self-actualization** is "an ongoing process" (p. 44) that involves making choices. In every moment, a person can choose to make a **regression choice** or a **progression choice**. "At each point," he wrote, "there is a progression choice and a regression choice. There may be a movement toward defense, toward safety, toward being afraid; but over on the other side, there is the growth choice" (p. 44). At every turn of talk, people can choose "to lie or to be honest" (p. 44), to conceal or to reveal, to withdraw or to move in the direction of another person. And, as I propose in this section, a person can choose to compliment rather than criticize. To proceed, the second part of the chapter introduces complimenting as an example of positive communication that affects others' development. The chapter ends by inviting you to observe your tendency to criticize and compliment, to study the use of compliments in everyday life, and then to practice complimenting more often.

Complimenting as Positive Communication

A **compliment**, according to scholars, "is a speech act which explicitly or implicitly attributes credit to someone other than the speaker; usually the person addressed, for some 'good' (possession, characteristic, skill, etc.) which is positively valued by the speaker and the hearer" (Telaumbanua, 2012, p. 34). Generally speaking, the function of complimenting is to make others feel good, but it sometimes serves a variety of other functions such as to reinforce solidarity, to encourage a desired action, or to soften an upcoming criticism. Researchers in the field of communication have shown the ways in which people in interaction "fish" for compliments (see Pomerantz, 1978) as well as how they respond to compliments. Some scholarship, for example, has revealed that although complimenting can serve positive functions, it can also threaten another person's sense of self (Brown & Levinson, 1978). Overall, though, researchers in language and social interaction have found that the central function of complimenting is to create and reinforce solidarity between and among people (see Wolfson & Manes, 1980). Compliments, in fact, can become some of the most memorable messages in a person's life.

Researchers across fields have shown the importance of complimenting in human relationships. In personal relationships, for example, we saw earlier how abusive couples tend to criticize one another while non-abusive couples tend to compliment each other much more often. Gottman (1994), who studied hundreds of couples in interaction, echoed this finding and found that criticisms in marital relationships foster a destructive pattern that leads couples into dissolution. Couples who are satisfied, however, exhibit what he calls the **five-to-one ratio**: for every negative act, there are five positive acts that compensate it. Based on his research, this ratio predicts "positive relational outcomes up to four years in the future" (Worthington & Drinkard, 2000, p. 99). In relationships at work, complimenting also matters. In the realm of education, for example, researchers have found that "positive statements (praise) have been found to be more beneficial than verbal criticism" in giving instructional feedback (Burnett, 2002, p. 5). Trees, Kerssen-Griep, and Hess (2009) found that feedback that communicates respect, liking, and mitigates threat is better received by students and directly affects their learning. In the workplace, Holmes and Marra (2004) showed how compliments made in passing, off-record, before or after a meeting helped to create team spirit and to construct good working relationships. In short, complimenting is a speech act that is important in everyday contexts: between lovers, with adults or children, with colleagues or employees, and at home or at work. It is an act of communication that is worth reflecting on, studying, and practicing.

Reflect on Complimenting. Complimenting is ubiquitous in social interaction. As we saw in this chapter, it is a speech act that matters in everyday relationships at home and at work. For this reflection, I invite you to pay attention to the way you compliment others as well as your tendency to criticize others. For the next five days, become aware of your own tendencies to compliment or criticize. Every day, write down in a journal any compliment and any criticism that you made. The purpose of this assignment is to simply observe your own behaviors in action and to reflect on your tendencies. During this period of observation, consider these questions:

1. How many compliments do you share with others on a daily basis?
2. How many criticisms do you make?
3. What do you compliment others about?
4. What do you criticize others about?
5. When is it most difficult for you to compliment?

Complimenting requires an interest in others as well as being able to see the positive in who people are and what they are doing. After five days of observation, write down three things that you learned about your own behavior and your tendencies. Then, study the behaviors of others.

Study Complimenting. Complimenting is an act of communication that can be studied empirically. Researchers have studied the use of complimenting in action. Wieland (1995), for instance, recorded dinner conversations between French and American speakers and studied the use of compliments in cross-cultural interaction. Other researchers have used interviews or surveys to understand how compliments are used and the functions they serve (see e.g., Al Falasi, 2007; Matsuura, 2004). Some studies have used ethnographic methods. Sifianou (2001), for example, collected 450 compliment exchanges in Greece to understand their various forms in the culture. For this study, I invite you to use a short survey to collect the best three compliments that people have received. The purpose of the survey is to understand the nature of memorable compliments in people's lives. Your goal is to ask eight people to write down three examples of compliments that they were given. This will give you 24 examples of memorable compliments.

Use the following short survey to collect your data.

Introduction
Every day, we all give and receive compliments. Some of the compliments we receive are particularly memorable and can help to define who we are as well as who we may become. Using this form below, please write down

the three most memorable compliments that you have **received** from others. After each compliment, please provide background to explain who gave you the compliment and how this compliment has affected you in the long term.

Compliment 1: _____
Context and Impact of the Compliment:

Compliment 2: _____
Context and Impact of the Compliment:

Compliment 3: _____
Context and Impact of the Compliment:

After you have collected all 24 compliments, write all of them down on a single page. Ask a few questions about the data: (a) What topic or content do the majority of the compliments focus on (e.g., appearance or ability?) (b) Who do the compliments tend to come from in memorable compliments? (e.g., family member or stranger?) and (c) What long-term consequences do the compliments have on the person? (e.g., improve self-esteem or provide an opportunity?). After examining all of the responses, write down three main findings from your study. Finally, identify your favorite compliments and share the stories with others.

Practice Complimenting. Several years ago, I met with Mr. Jensen, my professor at the University of Northern Iowa, to celebrate good news about my future. We sat in his office and I explained the graduate assistantships I received to pursue graduate school and my excitement. After listening carefully, he paused. Then, he said: "You know, Julien, all of this success is something which you have created." This is a memorable compliment that I have received. Today, I appreciate it even more because of the way the message was designed and its implications. In this compliment, he focuses on my engagement in the process, not the outcome. The compliment also foregrounds my agency in the process of success. This compliment illustrates what recent research would encourage all of us to practice.

When people perform well, there is a natural tendency to compliment or praise their abilities or talent. The instinct is to applaud their intelligence, talent, or skill. Recent research, however, has shown that "praising children's intelligence harms their motivation and it harms their performance" (Dweck, 2006, p. 171). Dweck and her colleagues, for example, revealed that "well-meant praise for intelligence, which is intended to boost children's enjoyment, persistence, and performance during achievement, does not prepare them for coping with setbacks" (Mueller & Dweck, 1998, p. 50). When parents, teachers, or coaches compliment children's intelligence, children use the compliments to assess their own self-worth. It cultivates the desire to be seen as smart. The research also shows that complimenting intelligence teaches children that intelligence is fixed rather than flexible, orients them toward valuing performance rather than learning, and causes them to avoid "being challenged." In short, complimenting intelligence seems to have both short-term and long-term consequences.

Through their research, Dweck and her colleagues have shown that the most effective way is to compliment effort, that is, to focus on the hard work and engagement that a person is displaying in a particular practice rather than the outcome that is produced. As Mueller and Dweck's (1998) data revealed, children praised for hard work "chose problems that promised increased learning" (p. 48), held "a more incremental theory of intelligence as malleable" (p. 49), and respond to setbacks more effectively, seeing them as a natural part of learning. Complimenting effort rather than ability can lead to much more positive consequences.

The purpose of this practice is to enable you to compliment others with a focus on process. Your objective is to compliment effort rather than intelligence and process over outcome. Use any opportunity that emerges in everyday interaction to give a compliment, especially after a person has experienced success. These are examples of how to move your compliments in a productive direction.

Complimenting Outcome	*Complimenting Process*
"You are really smart."	"I applaud how hard you worked."
"You are a great writer."	"I admire that you write every day."
"Nice 'A' on your English test."	"You really studied for your English test."
"Great performance."	"You've been practicing so diligently."

Complimenting process is not easy. It requires a shift in perspective and focus. What is most admirable about people is the way they engage in the process of their art, the way they persevere through challenges and setbacks, how they take risks to learn something new or to create, and to persist in the long term. A book is a product, but it is writing every day that brings it to life. A dance can be magical, but the magic can only be accomplished by daily practice. In her study of 40 recipients of the MacArthur Award, a prestigious grant given to creative individuals, Shekerjian (1990) found that persistence, practice for the long haul, and engagement were key to producing creative work.

In complimenting process rather than outcome, we can nudge one another a little further on the continuum of learning.

Summary

The main premise of this chapter is that communication affects the self. To support this principle, I first introduced symbolic interactionism and three major concepts: (a) altercasting, (b) ossification, and (c) intertextuality. These concepts all emphasize the idea that the spoken word affects another person: who they are and who they become. Then, I explained that complimenting is an act of positive communication that exemplifies the best in all of us. The act of complimenting is based on the understanding that what we say affects others in a real way. When we compliment, we affect another positively and give each other the courage to become.

Further Reading

Agassi, A. (2009). *Open: An autobiography*. New York: Knopf.

Bakhtin, M. M. (1984). *Problems of Dostoevsky's poetics* (C. Emerson, Ed. and Trans.). Minneapolis: University of Minnesota Press.

Blumstein, P. (2001). The production of selves in personal relationships. In J. O'Brien & P. Kollock (Eds.), *The production of reality: Essays and readings on social interaction* (3rd ed.). Thousand Oaks, CA: Pine Forge Press.

de Saint-Exupéry, A. (2000). *The little prince*. (R. Howard, Trans.). Orlando, FL: Harcourt. (Original work published 1943).

Dweck, C. (2006). *Mindset: The new psychology of success*. New York: Random House.

Gallwey, W. T. (1974). *The inner game of tennis: The classic guide to the mental side of peak performance*. New York: Random House.

Harris, T. (1967). *I'm ok, you're ok*. New York: Harper Collins.

Maslow, A. (1971). *The farther reaches of human nature*. New York: Penguin.

Sabourin, T. C., & Stamp, G. H. (1995). Communication and the experience of dialectical tensions in family life: An examination of abusive and nonabusive families. *Communications Monographs*, 62(3), 213–242.

Stockett, K. (2009). *The help*. New York: Berkley Books.

Key Conceptual and Theoretical Terms

Symbolic Interactionism
altercasting

ossification
    couple identity work
intertextualization
reported speech
    direct reported speech
    indirect reported speech
authoring
self-actualization
regression choice vs. progression choice
compliment
five-to-one ratio

· 5 ·

POSITIVE COMMUNICATION
DEEPENS RELATIONSHIP

Prelude

Writing is a challenging act of communication. In his book *The War of Art*, Pressfield (2002) describes the problem that most writers face: "There's a secret that real writers know that wannabe writers don't and the secret is this: It's not the writing part that's hard. What's hard is sitting down to write. What keeps us from sitting down is resistance." Then, he describes what resistance is and how it can be overcome.

Resistance is "the enemy within" (Pressfield, 2002, p. 8). It is the force that prevents us from exercising our creative right and realizing our potential. As he wrote, "Most of us have two lives. The life we live, and the unlived life within us. Between the two stands resistance." Pressfield adds that resistance cannot be seen: "we experience it as an energy field radiating from a work-in-potential. It's a repelling force. It's negative. Its aim is to shove us away, distract us, prevent us from doing our work" (p. 7). Resistance, he explains, is a force that is often embodied as procrastination, and it is fueled by self-doubt and fear: "Remember our rule of thumb: the more scared we are of a work or calling, the more sure we can be that we have to do it" (p. 40). Resistance fights our best self. Perhaps, then, it can also materialize in our communication.

Every communicator has something deep inside of him or her that he or she wants to reveal, say, or do. As a student recently asked me: "Why is it so hard to say what we know in our heart is best to say?" The answer is resistance. And so, the only thing to do is to overcome it: to say what we feel, to express our love and affection, and to reveal ourselves anyways. We can communicate in spite of the internal forces that are preventing our best expression of self. Overcome resistance: "I'm in love with you," "I'm sorry," "You can do it," or "I believe in you."

Introduction

"For communication to have meaning it must have a life. It must transcend 'you and me' and become 'us.' If I truly communicate, I see in you a life that is not me and partake of it. And you see and partake of me. In a small way we then grow out of our old selves and become something new. To have this kind of sharing I cannot enter a conversation clutching myself. I must enter it with loose boundaries. I must give myself to the *relationship*, and be willing to be what grows out of it."

—HUGH PRATHER, 1970

Communication, by definition, involves the act of revealing pieces of who we are. When we communicate, we naturally provide information about our self, ideas, opinions, and thoughts. The stories we share, the questions we ask, and what we divulge to others simply reveals who we are. This process is called **disclosure**. When disclosure takes place, it releases and expands who we are and it also functions to nurture relationships. In many moments in our lives, we disclose without reflecting much. Sometimes, disclosure requires a great deal of courage and personal strength. This chapter begins with the principle that positive communication deepens relationships. In the theoretical knowledge section, I introduce three major communication theories of disclosure and two core concepts. In the second part, the focus is on improving how you practice disclosure. I invite you to observe your own behaviors when you disclose, to study its importance in relationships, and to practice self-disclosure.

Theoretical Knowledge

Self-disclosure is the act of revealing private information. It is defined as "any message about the self that an individual communicates to another" (Gibbs, Ellison, & Heino, 2006, p. 156). Overall, scholars have shown that disclosure builds and nurtures relationships, as well as creates intimacy. It is a fundamental part of the process of relational development and an act of communication that is consequential in romantic relationships, friendships, in the family, as well as in the workplace. Self-disclosure also affects relational satisfaction. In this section, I first describe three major theories that inform scholars' understanding of how disclosure works. Then, I focus on two forms of disclosure: (a) congruent disclosure and (b) courageous disclosure.

Three Theories of Disclosure

In the field of communication, there are three main theories that focus on the process of disclosure and its significance in interpersonal communication. The three theories are Social Penetration Theory, Relational Dialectics, and Communication Boundary Management Theory. This section introduces each theory and its core concepts briefly.

Social Penetration Theory, which was proposed by Altman and Taylor (1973), essentially suggests that disclosure fosters intimacy and that relationships progress "through ever increasing breadth (amount) and depth of disclosure" (VanLear, 1987).

To put it simply, strangers become lovers as they share more and more information and learn about each other; they slowly peel themselves throughout the relationship and thereby become closer. Every relationship is completely unique because of what, and how much, is disclosed. It is the combination of depth and breadth of disclosure that defines how close people are. By definition, **depth of disclosure** refers to "how personal the information communicated is" while **breadth of disclosure** is the "sheer number of topics discussed" (Mongeau & Henningsen, 2008, p. 366). As partners reciprocate increasing amount of breadth and depth in disclosure, they become closer and closer. Not all relationships move in a linear fashion. The process of revealing one's self is influenced by personal characteristics, the assessment of costs and rewards, as well as the situational context (see Baack, Fogliasso, & Harris, 2000). Overall, though, the theory shows that disclosure creates how intimate people are and how satisfied they might be in their relationship.

A second theory is **Relational Dialectics Theory (RDT)**, which emerged from the work of Baxter and Montgomery (1996, 1998). Relational Dialectics Theory begins with the principle that in all relationships, people manage dialectical contradictions in the process of relating. A **contradiction** refers to "the dynamic interplay between unified opposites" (1998, p. 4). Specifically, Baxter and her colleagues have shown that relational partners manage a variety of contradictions that are not solvable; that is, the tensions must be continuously managed through communication throughout the life of the relationship. One dialectical tension, for instance, is the tension between autonomy and connectedness. Partners need to balance the need for independence and the need for connection. As Hoppe-Nagao and Ting-Toomey (2002) explained, the **autonomy-connection dialectical tension** refers "to the degree of interdependence in the relationship, specifically the contradiction between the desire for the freedom to be independent and the freedom to be dependent" (p. 142). A second dialectic, which is central to relationship development, is between openness and closedness. The **openness-closedness dialectic tension** refers to "the desire to disclose and be open with the relational partner and the desire to be discreet" (p. 143). Each person must thus constantly manage whether to express or conceal information, to talk or not talk. It is this process, and how the partners handle this tension, that defines what the relationship is all about: how close people are, how intimate they become, and how satisfied they are in the relationship. Relational Dialectics Theory acknowledges the important role that disclosure plays in relationships, but it is the way people manage these tensions that creates its nature.

The third theory that attends to the process of disclosure is **Communication Boundary Management Theory (CBMT)**, which was developed by Petronio (1991, 2002). Much like relational dialectics, CBMT views the process of disclosure as inherently dialectical. But it also adds that information is a form of possession and its dissemination a choice. People in relationships thus create boundaries of disclosure. As Petronio (1991) explained, the theory assumes "that revealing private information is risky because there is a potential vulnerability when revealing aspects of the self" (p. 311). As a result, "individuals erect a metaphoric boundary to reduce the possibility of losing face and as a means of protection" (p. 311). The term that is used to describe this process is **boundary coordination**. The concept simply refers to "how individuals co-own and comanage private information" (Petronio & Durham, 2008, p. 314). To manage private information, CBMT argues that people draw on privacy rules to decide whether to reveal or conceal information. Basically, **privacy rules** are criteria that communicators use to figure out what to disclose, how much to reveal, or whether to conceal. A person's decision to disclose or conceal is affected by multiple criteria including the larger culture, the gender of the speaker, the person's motivation driving the communication, the context of the relationship (e.g., whether people are married or divorced), and an assessment of the risks and benefits (see Petronio, 2002). To summarize, CBMT is helpful for reflecting about the complexity of self-disclosure, especially the ways in which people make decisions about what to disclose and what not to disclose.

As one example, Golish and Caughlin (2002) used CBMT to understand young adults' use of topic avoidance in stepfamilies. The results of the study show that adolescents engaged in the "most topic avoidance with their stepparents, followed by their fathers, and then their mothers" (p. 97). Of the many topics that adolescents avoided, sex was the most commonly avoided topic across all relationships. The following are examples of other topics that the young adults predominantly avoided:

Talking about the other parent:	"I avoid talking about my mom (to her father) and what we do together, like when she takes me places or buys me things."
Deep conversations:	"I avoid everything with my stepdad. Our conversations are very short and surface level. I basically avoid everything deep and personal."
Money:	"I don't like to ask my dad if he will help pay for my schooling because he will get upset. He already pays for child support."

Golish and Caughlin's (2002) research also described the various reasons (e.g., privacy rules) that the young adults used for avoidance with their mothers, fathers, and stepparents. The main reason that was offered was **self-protection** from feelings of vulnerability. For example, one person said, "I'm scared to talk to him [dad] about sex because I don't want to ruin his image of me" (p. 95). Another reason that was cited was to protect the relationship or the person in the relationship, officially called **relationship-protection**. As one participant explained, "I don't want to hear my mom put down my dad. I like my dad and don't want to hurt him" (p. 95). The third most cited reason was conflict; avoidance of disclosure was done to avoid conflict, including to avoid being "the middle person" between the parents. As one interviewee put it, "There is a lot of tension between my parents. They fought all 15 years of their marriage. They bad mouth each other. It feels awkward to be in the middle" (p. 95). The research thus shows that young adults avoid disclosure to manage the complexity of stepfamily life and do so to protect themselves, the relationship, and to avoid conflict.

Interestingly, though, further research in stepfamily communication has shown that strong stepfamilies report more openness in their communication. In contrast, and as Golish (2003) showed, "stepfamilies having difficulty often revealed avoidant tendencies" (p. 69). As an example, compare these two narratives from stepparents:

Excerpt 1:

We're always trying to be thoughtful of each other, but we're not hiding anything either.... If there's something that bothers us, or uh, you know, I think we have, instead of blowing up at each other and having a temper tantrum, we respect each other enough to say what's on our minds, and also to listen to one another.

Excerpt 2:

I think the lack of verbal communication has played a big role in our family. Mostly it is complete disregard for the other person. It's more the nonverbal communication that has played an important factor because, like um, my body language or lack of greeting when he comes into the room.

Openness in communication is critical to creating a strong stepfamily. This is also true of traditional family life in which "open sharing" and "openly confronting issues" are critical to "creating feelings of connectedness" (p. 71; also see Kelley & Sequeria, 1997). Disclosing can be difficult and risky, but research often shows that it is valuable at home and at work (Pennebaker, 1997).

In this section, I described three main communication theories that focus on the process of disclosure. Often, disclosure is a choice to involve people in our lives. Yet, every person must decide how much to disclose and to what depth with each person they meet. In every relationship, partners must balance the contradictory needs of openness and closedness. And certainly, as CBMT emphasized, it is natural to avoid some topics of conversation. Each of these theories teach us the importance of disclosure, but they each miss a positive twist: When do people disclose at their best? What conditions make disclosure an act of courage? The next section provides an answer to these questions by introducing two forms of disclosure.

Forms of Disclosure

This section focuses on two forms of positive disclosure: disclosure that is congruent and disclosure that is courageous. Revealing ourselves often is a challenge, but I explain how disclosure can enable each of us to grow in a positive direction.

 Congruent Disclosure. The best kind of disclosure takes place when people are able to match what they feel on the inside with what they do on the outside. This is called congruence. In this section, I explain this concept to show that congruent disclosure deepens relationships.

Congruent disclosure, according to Rogers (1961), occurs when a person's actions match their inner experience; when a person is able to "listen acceptantly to what is going on within himself, and the more he is able to be the complexity of his feelings, without fear, the higher degree of his congruence" (p. 61). Congruent communication is the expression of the "accurate matching of experience with awareness" (p. 282). It is something that we often recognize in others:

> With one individual we recognize that he not only means exactly what he says, but that his deepest feelings also match what he is expressing. Thus whether he is angry or affectionate or ashamed or enthusiastic, we sense that he is the same at all levels— in what he is experiencing at an organismic level, in his awareness at the conscious level, and in his words and communications. (p. 283)

From the perspective of Virginia Satir (1976) congruence is simply about being emotionally honest. As she wrote, "Being emotionally honest is the heart of making contact." Emotional honesty can take place inside of us with our inner voice, but it can also be embodied in the act of communication.

Congruent disclosure involves several key elements. First, there is a great sense of authenticity and genuineness. The person's communication matches the person's personality and attitude. Second, there is a feeling that the person's communication is truthful and honest. Third, congruent disclosure is personal—it does not reflect the surface of a person and reveals his or her depth. Fourth, the person who is communicating is able to drop the masks of pretension. They simply reveal their humanness, the strength and fragility of being a person. In sum, congruent disclosure is authentic, genuine, truthful, honest, personal, and human.

People know it when they are congruent or experience congruency from others. It is visible when the masks that we wear to protect ourselves are momentarily dropped during interaction. In their research, for example, Baxter and DeGooyer (2001) collected written accounts of more than 200 participants to find examples of beautiful conversations that they had experienced and to understand the nature of beautiful communication. They called these moments **aesthetic relating**. From these stories, the researchers found that congruency was an important part of what made a conversation beautiful and meaningful. Consider these two excerpts (p. 8).

Excerpt 1:

We were working through a questionnaire about our relationship, answering perti-
nent to our separation for my time in the Peace Corps. We spent much of the time
talking about our relationship and where it was going in the near future. We discussed
our fears for what could possibly happen and our dreams for what might be possible.
We both cried, but it was as much from our fear of what the future may hold for us
as it was from a feeling of love that we were getting from the other person (I should
speak for myself only I suppose). I felt scared for what could happen to us, but I also
felt lucky to be in such a position in the first place. What made the conversation
beautiful, I think, was the total honesty we developed and the unashamed way in
which we showed our emotion—not something that happens daily for either of us.

Excerpt 2:

We were sitting next to each other on a couch, but slightly turned to face each other.
There was soft music playing on in the background, and a relaxed atmosphere pulsed
the room. We had been together for a little over a year, but ... there was a barrier
between us. He showed genuine interest in me—my fears, desires, and dreams—and
I felt like I could say anything. Over the night these roles of speaker and listener
changed several times, depending on who needed to talk at the time. By the end,
we felt closer than ever before, and it was a feeling that lasted past just the moment.

In both of these moments, the narrators reveal how each person in the relationship was able to lift the veil of distance and get closer through communication. Notice how the characteristics of congruency are part of the narrators'
descriptions. In excerpt 1, the narrator emphasizes that honesty was a key
role in shaping the conversation as well as "the unashamed way in which
we showed our emotions"; in other words, they were able to drop the masks
and allow themselves to be human in front of one another. In excerpt 2, the
narrators focus on the importance of genuineness and how they were able to
talk about something very personal: fears, desires, and dreams. Genuine communication enables people to get closer.

We naturally connect with congruent communication. When a person
communicates congruently, "we recognize that he not only means exactly
what he says, but that his deepest feelings also match what he is expressing"
(Rogers, 1961, p. 283). We can literally feel and experience congruent communication, whether it occurs in interpersonal situations or in public speaking. When an utterance is spoken with courage or truth, when it is personal,
authentic, or genuine, we can momentarily drop our defenses and allow communication to reach us, and sometimes change us.

Congruent disclosure can also enable connection in public speaking contexts. When disclosure is authentic, personal, and human, the audience can connect. This talk, delivered by Elizabeth Gilbert, the author of *Eat, Pray, Love* (to watch the talk, go to http://www.ted.com/talks/elizabeth_gilbert_on_genius.html), exemplifies this point well:

I am a writer. Writing books is my profession but it's more than that, of course. It is also my great lifelong love and fascination. And I don't expect that that's ever going to change. But, that said, something kind of peculiar has happened recently in my life and in my career, which has caused me to have to recalibrate my whole relationship with this work. And the peculiar thing is that I recently wrote this book, this memoir called "Eat, Pray, Love" which, decidedly unlike any of my previous books, went out in the world for some reason, and became this big, mega-sensation, international bestseller thing. The result of which is that everywhere I go now, people treat me like I'm doomed. Seriously—doomed, doomed! Like, they come up to me now, all worried, and they say, "Aren't you afraid you're never going to be able to top that? Aren't you afraid you're going to keep writing for your whole life and you're never again going to create a book that anybody in the world cares about at all, ever again?"

So that's reassuring, you know. But it would be worse, except for that I happen to remember that over 20 years ago, when I first started telling people—when I was a teenager—that I wanted to be a writer, I was met with this same kind of, sort of fear-based reaction. And people would say, "Aren't you afraid you're never going to have any success? Aren't you afraid the humiliation of rejection will kill you? Aren't you afraid that you're going to work your whole life at this craft and nothing's ever going to come of it and you're going to die on a scrap heap of broken dreams with your mouth filled with bitter ash of failure?" (Laughter) Like that, you know.

The answer—the short answer to all those questions is, "Yes." Yes, I'm afraid of all those things. And I always have been. And I'm afraid of many, many more things besides that people can't even guess at, like seaweed and other things that are scary.

The rest of her talk focuses on the creative process, but the opening enables her to connect with her audience. She immediately acknowledges her love and passion, and then describes her personal experiences with her recent success. Then, she discloses her fears. Her talk is personal. And it is in its personalness that audience members also can find themselves. Being personal facilitates interpersonal connection. As Satir (1976) wrote, "The power in congruence comes through the connectedness of your words matching your feelings, your body and facial expressions matching your words, and your actions fitting all. You come from a state of strength because all of your parts have flow with other parts. You are not blocking anything off." Congruent disclosure simply reflects this unblocking.

Congruent disclosure is an example of how we can communicate at our best. It exemplifies the strength to be vulnerable in everyday, or public, communication. Often, although not always, being congruent requires courage.

Courageous Disclosure. In some contexts, revealing ourselves to others takes courage. Originally, the word *courage* "means to stand by one's core" (Nepo, 2007, p. 61). Often, it involves overcoming fear. The philosopher Comte-Sponville (2001), for example, explained that courage is "not the absence of fear; it is the ability to confront, master, and overcome fear" (p. 51). Tillich (1952) wrote that **courage** is "self-affirmation 'in spite of,' that is in spite of that which tends to prevent the self from affirming itself" (p. 32). Or, said differently, "to be courageous is to persevere in our being" (p. 53). Courage, then, involves the will to be who one is in spite of fear.

Courageous disclosure refers to revealing private information in spite of fear and risks. Very often, the decision to disclose reflects a person's choice to affirm themselves in spite of fear. Therefore, the choice to disclose can exemplify the virtue of courage. In his work, the philosopher Michel Foucault once spoke about the greek concept of *parrhesia*. By definition, **parrhesia** involves speaking the truth when there are risks. As Foucault explained:

> When, for example, you see a friend doing something wrong and you risk incurring his anger by telling him he is wrong, you are acting as a parrhesiastes. In such a case, you do not risk your life, but you may hurt him by your remarks, and your friendship may consequently suffer for it. (1999, para. 14)

Other examples can qualify. Think of employees who "blow the whistle" in their organization, such as Jeffrey Wigand, who single-handedly fought against the tobacco industry (Seeger, 1997). Of course, he faced many consequences for his disclosure. He lost his job, his family was threatened and later fell apart under the pressure. But, he was called to do the right thing. Or, it may involve telling friends that a joke that perpetuates racism is not funny or telling one's father that a dehumanizing comment is inappropriate. But telling the truth can also involve some of our most beautiful moments. Telling another person that you love him or her is a risk. Being honest and truthful is a risk. These moments of disclosure require courage, too. Just as one example, consider this short moment between a brother and a sister. They are meeting at McDonalds.

Excerpt 5:

Julia:	What is wrong? You seem upset.
Robert:	I am upset.
Julia:	What happened?
Robert:	I'm going to tell you something, but I do not want you to tell mom and dad. You are the first person that I have told.
Julia:	Ok.
Robert:	Me and Laura are separated.
Julia:	Oh.
Robert:	I know it seems sudden, but it has been going on a while. I just needed to tell someone.
Julia:	Well, I want you to know you can always talk to me. You don't have to keep it bottled up.
Robert:	I was not sure how you would take it.
Julia:	You are my brother. I am always on your side.

In this encounter, Robert's disclosure involves overcoming a degree of fear, the fear to be judged negatively and to lose love and respect from the people around him. When he discloses the separation of his marriage, he is inherently showing trust and openness. He is taking a chance. This is what makes disclosure an act of courage.

Not all moments of disclosure qualify as an act of courage. From my perspective, the criteria are (a) telling the truth, (b) overcoming fear, and (c) affirming the self. One example of courageous disclosure is particularly well illustrated by the men and women who "come out" (see Dindia, 1996). Researchers have shown that disclosing one's sexual identity functions as an act of courage. Often, the coming-out process involves moving in the direction of accepting who one is internally and then moving in the direction of others. In this case, the disclosure involves telling others something personal, telling them the truth about the self, overcoming the fear of being judged or unloved, and affirming the self in spite of those fears. As Cain (1991) described, "Gay individuals, then, confront a dilemma…By choosing to be open, they risk being seen as different and being harassed or ridiculed; they may also risk losing friends, family ties, or their jobs" (p. 72). On the other hand, "secrecy may create a sense of distance in relationships or may lead them to feel they are dishonest with trusted others" (p. 72). Researchers who have examined coming-out stories found that this tension between disclosing and not disclosing is very real. Dindia and Tieu (1996), for example, quoted from one of their participants: "I want to tell—hard to lie—hate to lie. Something pulls the other way. I don't know what" (p. 17). Maybe, it is courage that "pulls the other way."

Self-disclosure is one of the most difficult, but important, communication behaviors in healthy interpersonal relationships. Speaking openly and truthfully to friends, loved ones, or professional colleagues aligns with the virtue of courage, especially when it also involves overcoming fear and affirming one's self. Revealing ourselves—how we feel, what we value, our hopes and dreams, as well as what we believe in—when our communication comes from our core, it actualizes our selves, but moves us even more closely to others. Learning to reveal ourselves is a process that takes faith in others. Fortunately, it also is a skill that can be practiced.

Practical Knowledge

"I must do these things in order to communicate: Become aware of you (discover you). Make you aware of me (uncover myself). Be ready to change during our conversation. And be willing to reveal my changes to you."

—HUGH PRATHER, 1970

Communication involves the ability to discover others (see Chapter 3) and the ability to reveal our self. Disclosure is an inherent and important part of the process of relating. Openness increases intimacy, closeness, and helps to create cohesiveness in family life. Often, the act of disclosure reflects a degree of personal congruency and is often an act of courage. In this sense, disclosing exemplifies positive communication.

Disclosing as Positive Communication

The process of disclosing is both a natural part of relational development and often a choice that requires courage, particularly when it advances the well-being of the speaker. Great moments of personal disclosure reflect a speaker's ability to speak from his or her core: from a place of authenticity, genuineness, honesty, and personalness. It also involves taking a personal stance to be who one is: to accept our past, the complexity of our emotions, and the challenges of understanding who we truly are. Disclosing is an act of positive communication.

Research on the topic of disclosure is clear: disclosing, or being open with others, has a range of positive consequences. In personal relationships, disclosure fosters connection, intimacy, and cohesiveness. It also correlates with satisfaction in romantic relationships (Dindia, 2000). Researchers also have found that the act of disclosing has a range of positive functions for the person who is disclosing, including improving well-being, mood, and physical and mental health. Researchers know, for example, that "disclosure of traumatic experiences such as sexual abuse, can thwart physical and mental health problems" (Petronio, Reeder, Hecht, & Mon't Ros-Mendoza, 1996, p. 182). Disclosure is particularly positive when it is personal, genuine, and authentic. It needs to be congruent with the inner workings of the mind and to nudge the self to say something that is needed for itself (its growth). Disclosing is thus a communication behavior that is worth practicing and paying attention to. It is an act of communication that is worth observing in everyday life, studying, and practicing.

Reflect on Disclosing. Even though disclosing is important, most people struggle with the process. There is sometimes even a tendency to withdraw disclosure. This is well illustrated by the story from a woman who finally revealed the abuse she suffered from her stepfather (Pennebaker, 1990, p. 28):

> I had always been close to my mother. The divorce had nearly killed her and she was so happy with Jock [the stepfather]. If she had known what Jock was doing to me, it would have broken her heart. I wanted to tell her so much…Looking back on it all, the very worst thing was that I couldn't talk to my mother anymore. I had to keep a wall between us.

In this brief story, the speaker is emphasizing an important point about disclosure: she wants to disclose, but chooses not to, even though it is the act of disclosure that eventually sets her free. We all experience resistance to reveal ourselves. There is no other way to combat the resistance than by actually making the move: to disclose. The more personal it is, the more difficult it will be to reveal. But, perhaps, it will be the most liberating, the most rewarding, and out of this process may grow stronger relationships.

The purpose of this exercise is to reflect about what happens when you engage in personal self-disclosure. To do so, we are going to use writing as a tool for expression because writing about emotional experiences has shown positive outcomes on personal health and "significant reductions in distress" (Pennebaker, 1997, p. 162). For this exercise, you need to write 15 to 30 minutes a day for three consecutive days. Find a place where you are comfortable and where you will not be interrupted. The writing is for you only and does not need to be shared with anyone. Follow these directions to start the process (see Pennebaker, 1997, p. 162):

> For the next 3 days, I would like you to write about your very deepest thoughts and
> feelings about an extremely important emotional issue that has affected you and your
> life. In your writing, I'd like you to really let go and explore your very deepest emo-
> tions and thoughts. You might tie your topic to your relationships with others, includ-
> ing parents, lovers, friends, or relatives, to your past, present, or your future or to who
> you have been, who you would like to be or who you are now. You may write about
> the same general issues or experiences on all days of writing or on different topics
> each day. Don't worry about spelling, sentence structure, or grammar. The only rule is
> that once you begin writing, continue to do so until your time is up.

After you have conducted the exercise, reflect about the activity. You may ask
yourself:

> "How did writing about these experiences change my perspective?"
>
> "How did the act of disclosure affect my well-being?"
>
> "What was difficult about disclosing? What was easy to write about?"

Sometimes, the strongest cue about what to say may be what we are most
afraid of. As we saw about resistance in writing in the prelude: "the more
scared we are of a work or calling, the more sure we can be that we have to do
it." This might be true of disclosure too: the more afraid we are to let others
know, the more it needs to be released and shared with others. Find your core
and then have the courage to let it go.

Study Disclosing. In the course of relationship, people's commitments
and degree of intimacy naturally changes. Some communicative events, such
as expressing love for the first time or revealing something personal, can increase commitment and intimacy. Some conversations, such as a conflict or an
expression of dislike, can decrease or end a relationship. This understanding is
well-captured by the concept of turning point. By definition, a **turning point**
is "any event or occurrence that is associated with change in a relationship"
(Baxter & Bullis, 1986, p. 470). The purpose of this study is to understand the
events that are related to positive and negative change in relationships. For
this project, you will ask four to six individuals to fill in a diagram, which is
called the Retrospective Interview Technique (RIT). The RIT "asks each individual respondent to identify all of the turning points in his or her relationship since time of first meeting, [and] plotting these points on a graph" (Baxter
& Bullis, 1986, p. 476). After each participant has plotted a relationship, you
can ask further questions about the specific turning point.

To proceed, first provide a copy of the following graph and directions to
each person.

Directions for Turning Point Graph

Please use this graph to describe any event that has changed your romantic relationship over the course of its life. Mark each turning point on the graph, label each event to express what happened, and show how it affected your commitment to your partner. After placing all of the key significant moments in your romantic relationship, you will be asked to explain what happened as the relationship progressed.

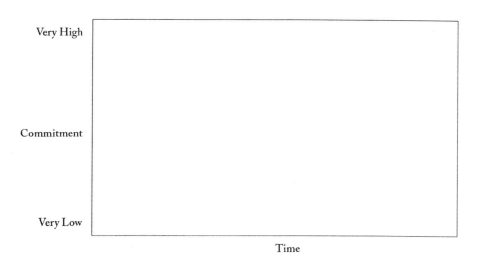

After collecting the graph, probe more deeply into participants' answers. For example, you may ask: (a) How did each turning point increase or decrease your commitment? (b) What was said during this turning point by you or your partner that influenced the relationship? (c) Which turning points affected most the development of your relationship?

After gathering the data from the graphs and conducting the short interviews, synthesize all of the information that you have collected to answer the following question: What turning points are more likely to increase commitment in a relationship? Write down the three main turning points that illustrate increased commitment. Share your findings with at least one person.

Practice Disclosing. Disclosing involves revealing information that is sometimes difficult, but it also involves sharing information that is positive. Letting people know that we love them is one example. Sharing how grateful we are for their influence on our life is another. This practice session is about expressing gratitude.

In his book on the great virtues, Comte-Sponville (2001) explains that "gratitude is a gift, gratitude is sharing, gratitude is love" (p. 134); "To thank is to give; to be gracious means to share. This pleasure that I owe to you is not for me alone. This joy, this happiness, they belong to both of us" (p. 133). No one accomplishes anything on his or her own. Gratitude is a person's understanding that other people contribute to his or her development. After all, no one is the cause of himself or herself.

This practice session is about expressing gratitude. Researchers in positive psychology have shown that expressing gratitude is one activity that raises people's sense of well-being and lowers depression in the long term. As Seligman (2011) wrote, expressing "gratitude can make your life happier and more satisfying" and can "strengthen our relationship with others" (p. 30). The purpose of this practice is to express gratitude and thereby raise your well-being, the well-being of a person you care about, and become a bit happier.

For this practice, please follow these easy steps (see Seligman, 2011):

Step 1:	Think of someone who is still alive who really contributed to your life.
Step 2:	Write a letter of gratitude to this individual. The letter should be about 300 words and should describe with great details what the person did for you and how it affected your life.
Step 3:	Call the individual and schedule a time for a personal visit. Be vague about the purpose of the meeting.
Step 4:	When you are face-to-face with the person, tell them that you want to read a letter for them. Read the letter (every word) aloud until you are completely finished.
Step 5:	After the letter, talk together about the experience.

Expressing gratitude is an act of positive communication. It produces good for you and another person. Self-disclosure can enable each of us to manage difficult emotions, but it can also enable us to bring us closer to the people we care about. Expressing gratitude is not necessarily easier than expressing an emotional experience: positive emotions sometimes make us even more vulnerable (see Brown, 2012). But when you disclose, you can deepen your relationships.

Summary

People are most afraid of closeness, not distance. Human relationships, however, are about intimacy and closeness. This is the challenge of the process of relating. In this chapter, I suggested that disclosing deepens relationships and exemplifies positive communication. The first part of the chapter increased your theoretical knowledge. To do so, I introduced three theories of disclosure: (a) Social Penetration Theory, (b) Relational Dialectics Theory, and (c) Communication Boundary Management Theory. Then, I exemplified two forms of disclosure: congruent disclosure and courageous disclosure. The second part focused on practicing disclosure. Disclosure is an act of courage because it reflects a person's own attempt for congruency and overcomes the fear that naturally comes with the process of relating. Revealing ourselves makes us vulnerable, but it strengthens our ties with others. By revealing ourselves, we can deepen our relationships with others and live more congruently.

Further Reading

Altman, I., & Taylor, D. (1973). *Social penetration: The development of interpersonal relationships.* New York: Holt, Rinehart and Winston.

Baxter, L. A., & Montgomery, B. M. (1996). *Relating: Dialogues and dialectics.* New York: Guilford Press.

Petronio, S. (2002). *Boundaries of privacy: Dialectics of disclosure.* Albany: State University of New York Press.

Prather, H. (1970). *Notes to myself: My struggle to become a person.* New York: Bantam Books.

Pressfield, S. (2002). *The war of art: Break through the blocks and win your inner creative battles.* New York: Black Irish Entertainment.

Rogers, C. (1961). *On becoming a person.* Boston, MA: Houghton Mifflin.

Seligman, M. E. P. (2011). *Flourish: A visionary new understanding of happiness and well-being.* New York: Free Press.

Key Conceptual and Theoretical Terms

disclosure
self-disclosure
Social Penetration Theory
    depth of disclosure
    breadth of disclosure
Relational Dialectics Theory
    contradiction
    autonomy-connection dialectical tension
    openness-closedness dialectic tension
Communication Boundary Management Theory
    boundary coordination
    privacy rules

    self-protection
    relationship-protection
congruent disclosure
    aesthetic relating
courageous disclosure
    courage
    parrhesia
turning point

· 6 ·

POSITIVE COMMUNICATION
GIVES SUPPORT

Prelude

Colors do not exist in the world. They exist in our mind. Our perceptions about people function similarly; they do not exist in reality. Perceptions feel real to us because they influence how we think. Unfortunately, they also affect how we act toward others in the present and in the future. Once we have formed an opinion of others, it is difficult for us to let it go. As the philosopher Jiddu Krishnamurti (1992) once explained in a talk:

> We all have opinions about people. We have a screen of ideas between ourselves and another person so we never really meet that person. If you see someone do something which you consider to be good or bad, you then have an opinion of him which tends to become fixed and, when you meet that person ten days or a year later, you still think of him in terms of your opinion. But during this period he may have changed; therefore it is very important not to say, "He is like that," but to say, "He was like that in February," because by the end of the year he may be entirely different.

Every person is growing, learning, and inherently changing. Sometimes, however, we assume that people cannot change or will never change. We can thus learn to renew our perceptions of the people around us. By renewing our perceptions, we can learn to see people as they are in the moment and to discover in them what we could not see before. If you want to renew your perceptions, try the following quick exercise:

> Choose a person that you know well but do not like right now or have a conflict with. Discover and write down 10 new things that are good about this person.

Introduction

"There are no ordinary moments."

—MILLMAN, 2000, P. 138

After surviving the concentration camps of World War II, Viktor Frankl (1984) wrote a groundbreaking book: *Man's Search for Meaning*. In the first part of the book, he narrates his experiences under the most devastating conditions facing humankind. He describes the dehumanizing process—what he saw and experienced. In the second part of the book, he describes a new therapeutic approach called **logotherapy**. The term simply means "therapy of meaning." More importantly, Frankl provided a point of reflection about how to find meaning in life. "The true meaning of life," he wrote, "is to be discovered in the world rather than within man or his own psyche" (p. 133). Specifically, he noted that meaning can be found in relationship. As he explained, "the more one forgets himself—by giving himself to a cause to serve or *another person to love*—the more human he is and the more he actualizes himself" (p. 133; emphasis added). This chapter focuses on one form of love: the way people support each other in times of crisis.

Whether during divorce, cancer, or the death of a family member, every communicator has at some point or another given or received support. This chapter argues that positive communication gives support. The theoretical knowledge part of the chapter supports this principle by describing research on social support. In the practical knowledge section, I propose that encouraging is a speech act that exemplifies positive communication, and that it is worth studying and practicing in everyday life.

Theoretical Knowledge

Researchers across disciplines have studied the process of social support. By definition, **social support** refers to "verbal and nonverbal communication between recipients and providers that reduces uncertainty about the situation, the self, the other, or the relationship and functions to enhance a perception of personal control in one's experience" (Albrecht & Adelman, 1987, p. 19). For Barnes and Duck (1994) social support includes all the "behaviors that ... communicate to an individual that she or he is valued and cared for by others" (p. 176). Said simply, social support involves communicating in a way that supports another person. For most researchers, social support has a positive impact: it nourishes the health of others and has a variety of positive physiological and mental consequences on both the recipient and the provider of social support. As Caplan and Samter (1999) explained, "[S]ocially supportive interactions are related to a variety of positive outcomes including reducing stress (e.g., moderating emotional and psychological distress), enhancing self-esteem, and providing tangible assistance with stressful experiences" (p. 245). Overall, researchers have consistently shown that social support has positive consequences on individuals' health (e.g., Kohn, 1996; Wright, 2002).

Social support is one important concept, but this chapter focuses more accurately on supportive communication. **Supportive communication** refers to "verbal and nonverbal behavior produced with the intention of providing assistance to others perceived as needing that aid" (MacGeorge et al., 2012, p. 212; also see Burleson & MacGeorge, 2002). Researchers have found that communication that is designed to offer support has positive outcomes as well. Psychologically, supportive communication has a "positive influence on ... confidence, self-efficacy, and self-esteem" (p. 216). It also has impact on a person's level of optimism and satisfaction with life. Most interestingly, supportive communication literally improves a person's health and his or her well-being. For example, researchers have found that "individuals receiving more high-quality emotional support tend to better resist disease onset, recover more quickly from various diseases and injuries, and maintain their health for more extended periods, and live longer" (p. 216). Finally, researchers have found that supportive communication has positive consequences on relationships. Scholars have found that "receiving high-quality supportive communication improves satisfaction and stability in marriages and other long-term romantic relationships" (p. 217; also see Cutrona, Russell, & Gardener, 2005). Basically, the research is clear: supportive communication carries positive consequences and functions as "the cornerstone for the quality of human life" (Albrecht, Burleson, & Sarason, 1992, p. 149).

Supportive communication is simply something "that others can provide when life events, whether big or small, create emotional distress and challenge our ability to cope" (MacGeorge et al., 2012, p. 212). Supportive communication can be performed in many ways. One form of supportive communication is called instrumental support. **Instrumental support** involves communication that provides information to assist another person. Sharing information, giving advice, or providing instructions are some examples of instrumental support. **Emotional support**, which refers to "communication behaviors intended to reduce emotional distress of others," is a second way of giving support. A third type is called **esteem support**. In this case, communication messages are designed to "enhance how recipients feel about themselves and their attributes, abilities or accomplishments" (MacGeorge et al., 2012, p. 221). Together, thus, everyday communicators have a variety of ways of giving support to others. In the rest of this section, I illustrate these forms of support by focusing on advice-giving in everyday interaction (instrumental support), the ways in which interactants give comfort and affection (emotional support), and how we give each other courage (esteem support).

Instrumental Support

Giving advice is one way to provide instrumental support through communication. By definition, **advice** is any "message that makes recommendations about what to do, think, or feel, in response to a problematic situation" (MacGeorge et al., 2012, p. 220). These messages make up 72% of the memorable messages that people recall as having a significant impact on their life. In one study, for instance, Knapp, Stohl, and Reardon (1981) reported that 42% of memorable messages contained advice about how the recipient could improve his or her self-concept—for example, "if you don't love yourself, no one else will" or "You can be whatever you want to be"" (p. 33). In their study, the authors also showed that most memorable advice giving came from a higher status person (a boss, a parent, or someone older). Overall, most of the memorable pieces of advice focused on getting along with others and on education or a job (e.g., "your vocation") and 90% of the recipients of memorable messages believed that the "message had a long-term, positive effect on their life" (p. 34). In short, an advice can be memorable and impactful in the life of the recipient.

In the book *Papa, My Father*, Leo Buscaglia (1989) illustrates that a father's advice can have long-term impacts. The book provides a portrait of his father and what he learned from him throughout his life. In one story, Buscaglia describes his own father's advice about how to appreciate wine:

Papa always prefaced the dinner with a dissertation on "the wine experience." This ceremony called for his finest wine, which had been aging in his modest but efficient wine cellar. Drinking wine, he would remind us, was a highly respected activity, not to be taken lightly. The nectar of the grape had brought joy to human beings long before recorded history.

"Wine is a delight and a challenge and is never meant to be drunk quickly. It's to be savored and sipped slowly," he'd tell us. "All the senses are awakened when you drink wine. You drink with your eyes, your tongue, your throat, your nose. Notice the colors the wine makes in the glass—all the way from dark purple, like a bishop's robe, to the golden amber of an aspen leaf."

This moment obviously stands in Leo's memory as a critical, life-enhancing moment. In his book, he adds that this piece of advice helped him in another situation and gave him the confidence to handle wine tasting with others.

An advice often emerges spontaneously in human interaction. The advice, then, can be a way of giving feedback, strength, and encouragement. In a series called *Comedians in Cars Getting Coffee*, Jerry Seinfeld takes a comedian out for coffee and simply relates on a number of topics. In one episode (see http://comediansincarsgettingcoffee.com), Jerry picks up Michael Richards, who played the role of Kramer in *Seinfeld*. At a coffee place, they sit down and reflect on life and the characters that animated their lives for years. Jerry makes a point and listens to his co-star:

Jerry:	But that was not our job. Our job was not for us to enjoy it. Our job was for us to make sure that they enjoy it. And that's what we did.
Michael:	Ahhh, you know that's beautiful. That's beautiful because I think I worked selfishly and not selflessly. It's not about me.
Jerry:	No.
Michael:	It's about them.
Jerry:	Yes!
Michael:	Now, that's a lesson I learned 7 years ago when I blew it in a comedy club.
Jerry:	Right.
Michael:	I lost my temper because somebody interrupted my act and did some things that hurt me and—
Jerry:	Right.
Michael:	—and I lashed out in anger.
Jerry:	Right.
Michael:	I should have been working selflessly that evening. Most of the time, when I'm in that zone, I am selfless.
Jerry:	Right. You told me that you had done a couple sets.
Michael:	No.

Jerry:	Do you want to?
Michael:	Sometimes I say I must, I should. And normally I would have gone in, and played around with some material, but no. I busted up after that event. It broke me down. It was a selfish response. I took it too personally. I should have just said, yeah, you're absolutely right, I'm not funny, I think I'll go home and work on my material and see you tomorrow night or something, anything. But, it's just, you know, one of those nights and thanks for sticking by me.
Jerry:	There was no issue with that.
Michael:	No really. Well, it meant a lot to me.
Jerry:	That's nice.
Michael:	But inside, it still kicks me around a bit.
Jerry:	Okay, that's, you know—
Michael:	That's a personal—
Jerry:	That's up to you.
Michael:	That's a big—
Jerry:	That's up to you to say: Well, you know, I've been carrying this bag enough.
Michael:	Yeah.
Jerry:	I'm going to put it down.
Michael:	Yeah. Yeah.
	(Both look at each other in silence)

Jerry's advice is designed to help Michael be a bit more gentle with himself. His advice, to put down the bag that he has carried long enough, provides Michael with a new perspective. Friends often can give each other the advice that is most needed and serve as our best therapists.

People can help one another cope with the challenges ahead. In one study, Holladay (2002) explored memorable messages about aging. By definition, **memorable messages** are "verbal messages which may be remembered for extremely long periods of time and which people perceive as a major influence on the course of their lives" (Knapp, Stohl, & Reardon, 1981, p. 27). In her study, she focused on messages that involved advice given by older individuals to younger persons about how to approach the process of getting older. Holladay found that many of these messages were positive. For example, the most significant number of advice-giving messages were encouragements to think of aging as a time of relaxation and contentment (Holladay, 2002, p. 696): "Don't be afraid to grow older. Growing old is an honor," "there is nothing better than growing old," or "Aging is a positive thing because it is when you begin to enjoy life to its fullest." A large portion of the advice reported was to enjoy life: "Live each day to the fullest and do everything you wish to do" or "make memories and enjoy life." Much of the content of the memorable advices was to encourage recipients to develop a positive mindset about aging. For example, participants in the study reported the following examples: "You're only as old as you feel," "I can be 80 and I will still act like a kid," and "getting old and being old are two different things" (p. 696). Holladay also found memorable messages to warn recipients that aging involves physical and cognitive decline, loss and loneliness, but that aging also is a natural part of life. In her data, Holladay found that the advice-giving carried both positive and negative consequences. In the positive side, the advice led recipients to think of aging more positively. As one person reported, "The message had a tremendous effect on my thoughts of old age. I now see old as an award for leading a decent life" (p. 692).

Advice-giving exemplifies that communication is an act of giving. Advice can shape our thinking, improve our connections with others, and help us make life-altering decisions. Smith and Ellis (2001), for example, showed that memorable messages serve as a "foundation for personal standards and morals" (p. 155) and that they are used to assess one's behavior after violating one's personal expectations. In this context, the most memorable messages were advice given about kindness, loyalty, and patience (e.g., "be patient with others," or "be helpful"). Memorable advice is often given by someone who is viewed as an authority figure such as a parent, a higher status employee, a trainer or a manager, as well as a teacher. Coaches also play an important role. In one study, Kassing and Pappas (2007) found that athletes reported a significant communicative influence from high school coaches. These are examples of memorable messages that the participants in the study reported:

> "The only one who can tell you that you can't do something is you. And you don't have to listen."

> "Someone is going to win. Someone is going to lose. If you lose, pick yourself up, dust yourself off, and go back at it again. This is life."

> "After all is said and done, you need to be able to look yourself in the mirror and know you have left it all on the field."

Advice can change a person for the better, encourage, teach, or form the foundation of a person's character. Communication researchers also have shown that giving advice can be dilemmatic (Goldsmith & Fitch, 1997). Giving advice can be viewed as "helpful" and "caring," but it can also be seen as "butting in" and intrusive. For those who give advice, there is sometimes a dilemma between being supportive and being honest. Not all pieces of advice function positively, but it is nevertheless the case that it is a way of giving to others. Often, as we saw in the section, advice is memorable and serves functions in the present and in the future. In the next section, I focus on how communicators can give by providing emotional support.

Emotional Support

Emotional support includes any communication behavior designed to reduce emotional distress. This section describes two forms of emotional support that exemplify the ways in which communication is an act of giving. The first is comforting communication. The second is affectionate communication. For each, I define the concept and provide examples to illustrate.

Comforting Communication. When the challenges of life take over, the strongest and healthiest response is to have someone to talk to so that they can comfort us. Comforting others is a crucial way to give to others. By definition, **comforting communication** refers to "any message that is designed to alleviate the suffering of others" (MacGeorge et al., 2012, p. 218). Research shows that the most effective way of giving comfort is to offer messages that are high in person-centeredness. Typically, **high person-centered comforting messages** have the following key features (see MacGeorge et al., 2012, p. 218; Burleson, 1982):

1. They explicitly acknowledge and legitimate another person's feelings by helping to articulate those feelings.
2. They elaborate on reasons why the other might feel that way.
3. They try to place the feelings within a broader perspective.

These three features are well-displayed in this communication moment. Recently, I played tennis with my good friend Joe. Tennis is the place we compete but also the place where we support each other. I was a bit fragile one morning. We're on the tennis court and I stop play. I come close to the net and I unleash. First, he listens. He initiates a few touches on the shoulder to give me support. He gives me the space to express myself. When I'm empty, he makes a few comments: "What you're experiencing is completely normal." He adds, "You're building a new relationship, a new commitment." Then, he provides perspective: "You're probably feeling caught between two windows: the window of your past and the window of your future." "There is always fear in moving forward, but you can do it." "I know this," he says, "it's going to be okay. You're going to find your balance." He gives me a hug. I'm comforted now and move back to the baseline.

In this moment, Joe acknowledges my experiences and provides a framework for making sense of them. He uses the "window" metaphor to help me understand my own experience. Then, he provides several reasons to legitimize my feelings and he places them in a broader framework. He is thus offering high person-centered comforting messages. In addition, he is also providing nonverbal comfort. He is hugging me, smiling, and staying close to me at the net. According to researchers, Joe is displaying the two primary elements that exemplify effective emotional support: (a) **verbal person-centeredness** and (b) **nonverbal immediacy**. The first concept, verbal person-centeredness, is defined as "the degree to which a support giver verbally expresses empathy and validates the distressed person's feelings" (Jones & Guerrero, 2001, pp. 567–568). Nonverbal immediacy "encompasses behaviors such as smiling, eye gaze, and direct body orientation, which reflect empathy, interpersonal warmth, and psychological closeness" (p. 568). Joe's emotional support illustrates well these two important processes.

Through communication, people can give comfort and enable a person to cope with the challenges of life. Comforting communication involves both talk and touch. Often, it involves expressions of love. At its peak, it becomes affection.

Affection Communication. A third important way through which we give emotional support to others is through **affectionate communication**. According to Floyd and Deiss (2012), "whereas affection is something we feel, affectionate communication is something we do" (p. 129). We do it by speaking words of love and through nonverbal behaviors such as hugging, kissing, and holding hands. Both of these are equally important ways of showing affection with people in our lives. Research has shown that being affectionate increases the quality of life, the quality of relationships with others, and our ability to cope with stress and challenges. As Floyd and Deiss reported, "highly affectionate people reported greater levels of happiness, self-esteem, and comprehensive mental health" (p. 132; also see Floyd, 2002). Affectionate communication is beneficial both when it is initiated and when it is received.

George Carlin, the infamous comedian, fell in love again after being widowed. Although he is well-known for his wonderful sense of humor and for his ability to create laughter, Carlin also created a second love story marked by daily notes of affection. Every day, he expressed his love for his wife until he died 10 years later. In her book, *The George Carlin Letters: The Permanent Courtship of Sally Wade*, Sally Wade (2011) describes their great love story and features what they wrote to each other, often on sticky notes. These are two of my favorites:

> "I'm so in love with you I could burst—but I promise to clean up the mess."

> "Sweet rose of my heart—I'm only about 20% of myself without you—I'll be home soon to claim the other 80%. I can't tell ya how much I miss ya. I love you with all my heart, and I always will. Love, love, love. Geo."

Next to the note, he added the drawing in Figure 6.1:

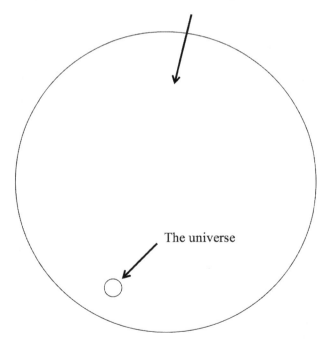

Figure 6.1. Note from George Carlin to Sally Wade (Adapted from Wade, 2011).

Affection can be expressed between lovers, but it also is crucial in family life and between parents and children. One type of relationship that often suffers from lack of affection is the one that takes place between fathers and sons. The research on father-son relationship has focused on the negative aspects of this relationship, even though men's and boys' relationships with their fathers "might be among the most influential and socially significant same-sex relationships that they have in the life course" (Floyd & Morman, 2003, p. 599). However, communication scholars have found that "affectionate communication is strongly associated with both fathers' and sons' feelings of closeness to each other and their satisfaction with their relationships and with their communication" (p. 601; also see Floyd & Morman, 2000; Morman & Floyd, 1999). In a review of the literature, Morman and Floyd (2002) explained that the father-son relationship is an important predictor of sons' future communication behaviors, relational success and communication with their spouses, attitudes toward sexuality, academic achievement, future income level, parenting style, potential for delinquent behavior, and overall emotional health. And yet, fathers and sons often find it difficult to "maintain positive, emotionally available relationships with each other" (p. 397).

In his book *Papa, My Father*, Buscaglia (1989) celebrates the many facets of his late father and his influence on who he became as a person. In an introduction to one of the chapters, Buscaglia quotes John Ritter, an actor and comedian:

> The last time my dad and I were together I was in Nashville, where he and mom lived. The two of us were in the car. He was driving, in his cowboy hat and coat. We were enjoying the moment. Then I looked at him chewing on his pipe, and was suddenly deeply moved. I had to say what was in my heart. It took a lot of nerve for me to speak up because he was so reserved. I said, "I just want to thank you for being my father. I think you're the greatest man I ever met and I love you." He smiled slowly before he said, "Yes, son, that's very nice." "Dad, I'd like to hear you say it, too." "What?" "Do you like me?" "Well, I love you." "Then, let me hear it." And he did. Three weeks later he was gone.

In the chapter, Leo Buscaglia (1989) describes the many ways his own father expressed love and affection, and how it bonded them closely. He recalls, "outward expression of affection was never a problem in our home" (p. 102), and describes some of the affection that he received from his father:

> One place we could always be assured of hugs was on Papa's lap. It was a royal area where we could find security and peace to be found nowhere else.... At times, he'd brush my hair with his hand or lean over and kiss my head. (p. 103)

At the end of the chapter, he concludes with a memory of one of the last acts of affection that they shared:

> I can still remember the last time Papa and I shared our love. We were walking on the sand near the ocean at Waikiki. He looked old and tired, and his brisk walk was by now a slow, pained gait. I had an uncontrollable urge to stop right there and take him into my arms and hug him. But Papa, always the nurturer, spared me the trouble. He stopped and reached out to me, took me into his arms, and spoke the very thoughts I wanted to express. "Don't be sad," he said in Italian. "We've had a nice life together."

Affection is one way to give meaning to another person's life when it is *communicated*. Affection without communication may be real in a person's mind, but it cannot be experienced by another person unless it is made available with the spoken word or a soft gesture. This is why it is crucial to communicate affection to others. Social support is something we do, not just something we think about. Emotional support is one way to give to others. Esteem support is another.

Esteem Support

Esteem support reflects any verbal or nonverbal messages that affect another person's sense of self positively. As MacGeorge et al. (2012) defined it, esteem support "is a form of supportive communication provided to enhance how recipients feel about themselves and their attributes, abilities, or accomplishments in the face of an esteem-threatening event" (p. 221). This section illustrates forms of esteem support and proposes that encouraging is a crucial form of esteem support.

Social support groups provide an important context in which people come together to find support from others. Often, individual group members join to cope with a trauma, event, or health problem. Support groups have been formed to help individuals overcome alcoholism, divorce, or cancer. Today, many support groups take place online (see Wright & Bell, 2003). Through email or posts, people can listen to one another, express their pains, suffering, and successes, as well as provide support to others. In one study, for example, Mirivel and Thombre (2010) explored the textual narratives of an online support group called Surviving Together. The group was formed as a discussion list to provide a supportive space for burn survivors. Using email, the survivors contact each other to express their pain, describe the incident, give advice to one another, and support each other. In the data that were collected, group members often provided one another with esteem support through encouragement. Many of the encouragements, as shown below, were about overcoming issues of self-esteem and beauty.

Example 1:

Martha: Just know that you are still the better and stronger person for having come through this and you are BEAUTIFUL! ... You are a very strong, beautiful, incredible woman so hold your head up high and be proud of who you are.

Example 2:

Jessica: This morning, this raving burned beauty still got a kiss on the cheek from my husband John before he went to work. Some of you young folk are concerned about will you have love in your future. Keep a good attitude and wait patiently for the right person. You will attract the right person like a Phoenix to a flame. Everyone is not shallow or vain, there are really nice people out there and I have met a lot of them right here.

In both examples, the writer is encouraging other group members. In the first one, the encouragement is designed for a specific individual who was feeling down about her physical appearance. The encouragement is designed to help the other person improve the way she looks at her body. The second example is an encouragement for everyone. The message is designed to give listeners hope and encourage them to think about the future in a positive way.

Giving advice and complimenting are good examples of esteem support. But encouraging is a speech act that illustrates esteem support well. As Dinkmeyer and Eckstein (1996) defined it, **encouragement** is a "process whereby one focuses on the individual's resources in order to build that person's self-esteem, self-confidence, and feelings of worth" (p. 16). As a speech act, it can take place in every aspect of human interaction: at home and at work, as a parent or friend, a leader or mentor, a teacher or student. In education, leadership, and parenting, encouraging is seen by scholars across disciplines as an act of communication that is influential (e.g., Carns & Carns, 2006). Encouraging serves many functions including "to inspire with spirit, to foster hope, to stimulate, to support, or to instill courage and confidence" (Pitsounis & Dixon, 1988, p. 509). Said simply, encouraging exemplifies an important way through which we can give to others.

Being encouraged matters. Eckstein and Cooke (2005), for example, interviewed more than 1,000 couples to understand the nature of encouraging behavior. They asked couples to interview one another about moments in which they were encouraged. After collecting all of the stories, the researchers revealed seven methods of encouragement. Encouragement came from role models, from someone revealing their strengths as well as their weakness, from having someone being consistently present over the long term, from being seen as special in some way, by being inspired in moments of crisis or difficulty, by supporting a person's endeavor, and by encouraging specific career choices. The following are examples of encouraging messages that participants in the study reported (see Eckstein, 2012):

> "Virginia, people can take away your house, your job, take away everything but they cannot take away your education." (p. 17)

> "You have the skills to do this. I've seen you with these boys and you have a good rapport with them. I'm confident that you'll do just fine; just trust yourself." (p. 18)

> "If you put forth your best effort, you can make it happen." (p. 19)

> "Never quit. Size means nothing." (p. 21)

> "I'm in your corner, and I always will be!" (p. 21)

Each of these messages had a profound impact on the recipient. Each story is a reminder that "Encouragement is one of the practical building blocks that can help bridge the gap between our potential and our self-imposed limitations" (Eckstein, 2012, p. 14). Encouraging is an important way to give support to others.

This major section introduced three important forms of social support: (a) instrumental support, (b) emotional support, and (c) esteem support. For each type, I provided examples to illustrate how social support is done in everyday communication. Research on supportive communication has shown that it is essential in personal and social relationships and that social support illustrates our capacity for strengthening another, helping others overcome themselves or a crisis, and enables each of us to cope with the uncertainties of living. The speech act of encouraging is particularly crucial. No one accomplishes anything alone. We need other people to give us the courage to become. It is an act of communication that is essential to the practical art of communication.

Practical Knowledge

"People are both actuality and potentiality."

—Maslow, 1971

The first part of the chapter introduced the theoretical background to understand how social support functions in human interaction. In this part of the chapter, I focus on improving the way you practice social support. Our attention is on the speech act of encouraging because it exemplifies positive communication.

Encouraging as Positive Communication

In each of us, there is who we are now, in the present moment, and who we are capable of becoming, our potentiality. Encouragements function as a bridge between these two selves. It exemplifies a communicator's ability to imagine in others what they may not see in themselves. It is through encouragements that an individual's potential is realized. In this way, encouraging functions as a crucial example of positive communication.

Encouraging, like other forms of social support, has a range of positive outcomes. In their review of the literature, MacGeorge et al. (2012) explained that high-quality supportive communication affects others' psychological health, including confidence, self-esteem, the capacity to cope with challenges, and the ability to make decisions. Quality support also has physical outcomes. An encouragement can enable a person to make better health choices or to decrease anxiety. As I mentioned earlier, "individuals receiving high-quality emotional support tend to better resist disease onset, recover more quickly from various diseases and injuries, maintain their health for more extended periods, and live longer" (p. 216). Third, supportive communication enhances all kinds of relationships: friends, families, and coworkers. Encouraging is one important way to have a positive impact on others.

Often, though, encouraging requires a proper mindset. In the field of psychology, researchers have pointed out that encouraging is a way of seeing; it is deeply connected to our ability to see potential in others. As Li, Lin, Lai, Eckstein, and Mullener (2011) explained, "To encourage is to realize that although there are negative and positive emotions, ultimately it is one's own perception that makes a profound difference" (p. 893). "Encouraging individuals," the authors wrote, "have the ability to perceive a spark of divinity in others and then to act as a mirror that reflects that goodness back to them" (p. 893). Encouraging is a positive act of communication, first in the sense of seeing potential in others, and second in the sense of making that potential come to life. It is an act of communication that is worth reflecting on, studying, and practicing.

Reflect on Encouraging. In 2007, Lewis Pugh, an environmental campaigner and pioneer swimmer, swam across the North Cape to bring public focus to the melting icecap. Two years later, he delivered a Ted talk to describe how he prepared for the record-breaking swim and braved the ice-cold waters (see http://www.youtube.com/watch?v=HALd9FY5-VQ). On the way there, he lost hope while wondering how he was going to survive 20 minutes under these conditions. In the talk, he then described what a close friend told him:

> And my close friend David, he saw the way I was thinking and he came up to me and he said: "Lewis, I've known you since you were eighteen years old. I've known you and I know, Lewis, deep down, right deep down here, that you are going to make this swim. I so believe in you Lewis. I've seen the way you've been training and I realize the reason why you're going to do this. This is such an important swim. We stand at a very very important moment in its history and you're going to make a symbolic swim here to try to shake the bells of world leaders. Lewis, have the courage to go in there because we are going to look after you, every moment of it." And I just got so much confidence from him saying that because he knew me so well.

After this talk, Pugh accomplished his goal successfully, swimming across the North Cape. His story illustrates that personal accomplishments are often tied to the people around us because they give us the courage to accomplish our dreams. This courage is given to us through communication. With the spoken word, people can give us the strength to actualize our best self.

Encouraging is a speech act that improves another person's sense of self and enables that person to keep growing in the face of adversity, obstacles, or challenges. The purpose of this activity is to reflect about the importance of encouraging messages in your own life and to see how those messages may have helped you achieve practical outcomes.

Begin by making a list of five key accomplishments in your life. Those accomplishments can include anything that is important to you and that you believe required effort, practice, or focus for a significant amount of time. The accomplishment can be personal (e.g., quitting smoking or exercising), professional (e.g., earning a degree or getting to a desirable position), or relational (e.g., getting engaged, ending a relationship, or having a child). List these accomplishments on paper in any way that you see fit.

With your list in hand, reflect on each accomplishment. Ask yourself as many questions as you can to bring yourself back to that specific time in your life. For example, you could ask: (a) How did I reach this success? (b) What did I do to deserve this accomplishment? (c) How did I create it? (d) How did others provide support during that time? (e) What interactions were meaningful to me during the time? What is important is to reflect deeply on the whole experience.

After reflecting on each accomplishment, identify for each success an encouraging message that you received from someone. Then, write down the specific words spoken to encourage you. Each quotation, as exemplified below, should be aligned with the accomplishment that you listed.

Accomplishments:

1. Stop smoking	"You know how you stop smoking? You do it one cigarette at a time." (Colleague)
2. Earning my doctorate	"Julien, you can do this. You're almost there. What you have done is amazing. Let's finish strong." (Father)

The activity should help you recall specific instances of encouraging communication and to realize the importance that those messages have had on your life.

In short, words of encouragement matter. They function positively in human interaction and enable each person to nudge toward a healthier self. As we saw earlier, courage is the ability to overcome fear. Encouraging is any form of communication that is designed to help others overcome the fear of becoming. After reflecting on your own experience, you can now study the experiences of others.

Study Encouraging. Most individuals have either received some form of encouragement or given others some words of encouragement. As we saw earlier, Cooke and Eckstein (2012) interviewed more than 1,000 individuals to collect their stories of encouragements. This activity will introduce the method that the authors used to collect those narratives. The purpose of this activity, then, is to see the importance of encouragement in people's lives. To do so, you will collect eight encouragement stories from anyone in your personal circle of acquaintances. To collect those stories, you will conduct short interviews with each person. As Cooke and Eckstein (2012) explained, "The objective of the interview activity is to help the subject re-call a person or an event from which they drew encouragement" (p. 15). To collect the stories, use Table 6.1 and write down your participants' answers:

Table 6.1. Encouragement Story Template (from Cooke & Eckstein, 2012, p. 16)

The Recollection	Your Response
The person (or source) of the encouragement was …	
If the source was a person, what is your relationship to the person who encouraged you:	
What the person said about you or to you:	
What was the situation in which the encouragement occurred?	
Your age at the time of the event:	
Looking back, how does this encouragement relate to the person you have become?	

After conducting the eight interviews, look for themes in the information that you gathered. You may ask these key questions to guide your thinking: (a) What do the encouragements tend to be about? (b) What functions do they generally serve? (c) What impact do the encouragements have on the recipients? Then, using these questions, develop three main findings from your interviews. Write these three findings down and share them with at least one person. Then, use the stories as an inspiration to encourage others.

Practice Encouraging. Encouraging others involves being attentive to the potential in others. It can contribute to the welfare of others and can strengthen them in a moment of self-doubt. The purpose of this practice session is to deliver one encouraging message to one person *today*. This person can be a student, a friend, a lover, or a colleague. Before delivering the message, proceed in this way:

1. Identify the person who you would like to encourage.
2. Reflect on the person's potential: What do you see as being the person's strength? What do you think the person could accomplish with your support? What can he or she become?

3. Write down the message that you want to deliver.
4. Deliver the message: "I've been thinking of you today. I believe that you are an amazing person and that you can accomplish anything that you set your mind to ..."

This activity is an invitation to encourage one person, but encouragements can be practiced on a daily basis. Reach for the people around you and strengthen them when they need it most. Share what you see in them, the vision they may not see in themselves, and tell them that you believe in them. Through encouragements, we can nudge one another toward our potential.

Summary

In this chapter, I argued that positive communication gives support. Through communication, we can give advice, support, affection, comfort, and encouragements. Supportive communication enables others to overcome a crisis, change the direction of their lives, reach for a person's success, and give the courage that all of us need to accomplish anything that is of value. In the first part of the chapter, I unpacked the research that is available on the concept of social support. In the second part, I invited you to observe the impact that encouragements have had on your life, to listen to others' stories about encouraging behavior, and to practice the speech act even more frequently. Encouraging is an act of positive communication that enables us to strengthen each other and help us move beyond our personal limits.

Further Reading

Burleson, B., & MacGeorge, E. (2002). Supportive communication. In M. K. Knapp & J. A. Daly (Eds.), *Handbook of interpersonal communication*. Thousand Oaks, CA: Sage.

Buscaglia, L. (1989). *Papa, my father*. Thorofare, NJ: SLACK.

Floyd, K. (2002). *Communicating affection: Interpersonal behavior and social context*. Cambridge, UK: Cambridge University Press.

Frankl, V. (1984). *Man's search for meaning*. New York: Washington Square Press.

Millman, D. (2000). *Way of the peaceful warrior: A book that changes lives*. Novato, CA: New World Library.

Wade, S. (2011). *The George Carlin letters: The permanent courtship of Sally Wade*. New York: Gallery Books.

Key Conceptual and Theoretical Terms

logotherapy
social support
supportive communication
instrumental support
    advice
    memorable messages
emotional support
    comforting communication
        high person-centered comforting messages
        verbal person-centeredness
        nonverbal immediacy
    affectionate communication
esteem support
    encouragement

· 7 ·

POSITIVE COMMUNICATION TRANSCENDS SEPARATENESS

Prelude

Close your right hand and make a tight fist.
Feel the tension in your arm and hand.
Now, slowly open your hand so that you palm faces up.
"This symbolizes the whole story of learning" (Baker, 1977, p. 5).
Learning is about opening your hand. It is about accepting.

Introduction

"The deepest need of man, then, is the need to overcome his separateness, to leave the prison of his aloneness."

—FROMM, 1956, P. 9

The beloved writer Leo Lionni (1959) once wrote a children's story called *Little Blue and Little Yellow*. In it, Little Yellow and Little Blue are close friends. They play together. One day, Little Blue leaves his house to find Little Yellow. When they find each other, they are so happy to see each other that "they hugged each other ... and hugged each other ... until they were all green." This chapter is about how people become green in communication.

Scholars offer many definitions of the word *communication*. Its roots, however, give us a reminder of the metaphor that its uses stand for. As Peters (1999) explained, "Communication is a word with a rich history. From the Latin *communicare* meaning to impart, share, or make common, it entered the English language in the fourteenth or fifteenth century" (p. 7). Communication simply means to make common: to bring the self and the other into a shared reality, to narrow the differences between who we are and what we could be, and to make ourselves one. Every person can relate to this point: by communicating with others, we create a shared field of experience and find ourselves in each other. In brief moments of true communication, we *become* pieces of another and find momentary comfort in mutual understanding. In these moments, we become "green."

This chapter argues that positive communication transcends separateness. The focus is on practices that foster dialogue, or great moments of human contact. Many scholars and thinkers use the word *dialogue* to describe moments of communication in which people are able to meet each other fully, respectfully, and experience shared understanding. The theoretical knowledge section explores the scholarship of Jiddu Krishnamurti, Carl Rogers, and Martin Buber, and a few other writers to define dialogic communication and exemplify its four main characteristics. In the practical knowledge section, I suggest that listening is the quintessential element of dialogic communication and a skill worth observing, studying, and practicing.

Theoretical Knowledge

"Without the ability to create moments that are beautiful, thrilling, and awe inspiring, life is empty."

—CRONEN, 1998, P. 22

It's a cold and rainy day. Classes were canceled earlier, so only five students show up for my class. I decide to start by just asking: "What do you guys want to talk about today?" For at least 20 minutes, we chitchat, do small talk. At some point, I ask: "What do you guys want to talk about in terms of interpersonal communication?" A few students comment, but then the conversation takes a turn. One student, Allison, describes the challenge she is facing. She says she is mothering her own siblings because her mother is absent, focused on her computer, and yelling at the small children anytime she hears a sound that feels disruptive. Allison feels responsible. She wants to reach her mother, but she doesn't know how. She describes her parents' separation and their lack of affection. She says: "How come the boys are eating their meals in front of the television in their room?" "Why don't we have dinner together?" She wants to make contact. The other students listen attentively and are completely focused on her. We're all feeling what she is describing. One student provides a few suggestions and encourages her. "You're doing wonderful. It's going to get better and you'll look back at this situation and will find that it strengthened you." Allison continues: "the boys should see what love and affection really looks like. They should see that a marriage can be loving." We pause, we see each other, we relate. Then, the student next to me says: "You know, being a mother and a wife who suffered from depression, I think I understand what your mother may be going through. Maybe, if my husband would have said, 'you're not yourself. I love you and you need to step out of it and seek help,' I think it would have made the difference." Later, another student adds: "I know exactly how you feel. I went through a situation almost exactly like yours." She describes what she went through. During our time together, without being conscious of it, we are making full human contact and creating a dialogue. We are briefly connected and transcend our differences.

This theoretical knowledge section focuses on how moments like this one emerge in the course of human interaction—how dialogue is created and what communication elements make it possible. First, the section introduces the concepts of dialogue and dialogic communication. Second, I illustrate the four main characteristics of dialogic communication.

Dialogue and Dialogic Communication

In human interaction, it is sometimes possible for people to meet each other fully, understand one another deeply, and make quality contact. Communication scholars and theorists define these moments as dialogue. Linell (1998) defined **dialogue** as "interaction through symbolic means by mutually co-present individuals" (p. 11), which involves "mutual attentiveness and responsiveness, shared focus, congruent plans, and social (communicative) objective" (p. 13). For the philosopher Martin Buber (1965), "There is genuine dialogue—no matter whether spoken or silent—where each of the participants really has in mind the other or others in their present and particular being and turns to them with the intention of establishing a living mutual relation between himself and them" (p. 19). For many scholars and researchers, dialogue represents the best form of human communication; it occurs when differences are transcended and people reach mutual understanding of each other. Dialogue is a short-lived moment of conversation. As Cissna and Anderson (1998) argued, "the qualities necessary for genuine dialogue occur only occasionally and for brief moments" (p. 68). Yet, in these moments, people come together more closely, overcome their differences, and create a context to discover each other more deeply, more humanely.

Dialogue "can't be forced, [but] it can be nurtured" (Isaacs, 1994, p. 374). Dialogue is what happens when people engage in a particular kind of communication process. This process is called dialogic communication. Simply defined, **dialogic communication** refers to any verbal and nonverbal messages that create the conditions for genuine dialogue to emerge. Dialogue is the outcome and dialogic communication is the process. Dialogic communication involves (a) openness, (b) unconditional positive regard, (c) empathy, and (d) genuineness. Each of these elements, when practiced by multiple individuals in interaction, co-create dialogue.

Openness. The first main characteristic of communicating dialogically is openness. Openness means to have no barriers. It involves the ability to freely express one's ideas, thoughts, and opinions. Openness, in the context of dialogic communication, more accurately refers to one's ability to welcome new ideas, new perspectives, and to be willing to change. As Cissna and Anderson (2004) explained, in dialogue "persons remain thoroughly open to the particular and unique perspectives of their partners" (p. 195). The philosopher Gadamer (1989) echoed this point when he wrote that without "openness to one another there is no genuine human bond" (p. 36). The task of openness is to be able to move in the direction of others, consider alternative perspectives, and discover new ways of thinking.

The challenge of dialogic communication is to remain "in the tension between holding your own perspective (and) being profoundly open to others" (Pearce & Pearce, 2000b, p. 162). To do so, a person must be willing to listen fully to another without judgments and evaluation. In his writing and speaking, the thinker Krishnamurti (1992) explained, "We should be able to listen to what is being said without rejection or acceptance. We should be able to listen so that if something new is being said, we do not immediately reject it." Carl Rogers (1961) aligned with this stance and proposed that the "major barrier to mutual interpersonal communication is our very natural tendency to judge, to evaluate, to approve or disapprove, the statement of the other person, or the other group" (p. 330). Later, he adds: "the great majority of us

could not *listen*; we would find ourselves compelled to *evaluate*, because l
ing would seem too dangerous. So the first requirement is courage, and w ˍ˳
not always have it" (p. 333).

Listening openly to others means that we welcome the possibility of
being influenced by them. Sometimes, it involves welcoming the possibility
of changing ourselves for the better. This point is well-displayed in an interaction between students about race (Poulos, 2008, pp. 125–126). This point
in the conversation emerged after watching Martin Luther King Jr.'s famous
"I Have a Dream" speech and much, sometimes uncomfortable, discussion.
As Poulos (2008) wrote, "Finally, what seems like a moment of breakthrough
comes upon us in the form of a simple invocation" (p. 125).

Mike:	(who identifies himself as black) Look, y'all are all racists. Joe said it, and I say it again. Why don't you just admit it?
Daniel:	(a "white American") I just don't know how you can say that. How do you know? You don't really know me, or us.
Mike:	(laughs) I don't just mean you white folks. I mean all of you. Y'all are all racists. Hell, I'm a racist. We still judge—we notice—skin color, as if that's what's different about us. You see me as black and that makes a difference in how you see me; I see you as white and I wonder about you.
Brent:	Oh, come on.
Kena:	(an "African American" student) I think we all need to listen to what Mike's saying. I think y'all are all jumping down his throat. You're arguing with him. You need to hear what he's saying. If we are going to have this conversation, you can't just keep denying what he's saying. You have to accept it as his point of view.
Mike:	Thanks for taking my back; I appreciate it. I really do. But I have to say that I enter this conversation because I want to come out of it a better person. If I change—or if any of us change—because of talking about this, then it's a good conversation. If we change because we're having it, we have succeeded, seriously. The fact that we are having this conversation is big, but we should do something with it. We don't have to agree. Just change. Change *something*.
Jessica:	(a white student, who identifies herself as "American") I think we all need to go out on a limb. We need to risk ourselves to see a new way to live together.
Christopher:	(white American male of Greek and Scottish descent) That's what I mean when I say we need dialogic courage. It takes some sort of risk, rising up out of the heartfelt sense of possibility that we might connect in some important way, if only we step beyond our com-fort, beyond our preconceived ideas, beyond our scripts, beyond our cultural chains.
Kena:	Yes. That's it. And first you gotta *listen*.

Listening openly is about letting people in. When people make full human contact, they are momentarily open to one another. They are letting each other in: either physically by getting closer or symbolically by allowing the influence of talk.

In one study, Montague (2012) interviewed participants to find out what their experiences with dialogue were like. After conducting the interviews, he found that many people expressed the importance of being open. In fact, Montague found that for most people, dialogue began with an invitation. As he argued, "The initial invitation is what encourages individuals to take a chance, to explore…it is a communicative offering" (p. 404). Often, the moment requires the persons involved to be open to the possibilities of communication. One participant, for example, describes how her dialogic moment was made possible:

> That was actually the very first time me and him had ever sat down, just the two of us, and had a conversation. And I think that the ability for us to interact the way that we did was definitely based on his openness and humbleness. It had a lot to do with like his humbleness, the flow of the back and forth, and his willingness to talk about things. (pp. 405–406)

As shown in this example, openness helped to create this moment of dialogue.

Openness is important in romantic relationships, but researchers have shown that it is crucial across many contexts. For example, openness is crucial in marriages. As Montgomery (1981) explained, "quality communication in marriage depends on bilateral openness." Openness also is a key characteristic of strong families and stepfamilies (Golish, 2003), an important facet of transformational leadership (Judge & Bono, 2000), and a vital aspect of intercultural competence. As Briede (2006) argued, "intercultural competence actually is a question of openness to difference" (p. 62). Openness also is crucial in health care. In one study, Dwyer, Nordenfelt, and Ternestedt (2008) argued that listening with openness is a critical part of how to care for the elderly people living in nursing homes. In fact, the most common complaint from patients about their doctor is that they do not listen (see Meryn, 1998). Listening openly also is a hallmark of great teachers (e.g., DeVito, 1986). In short, openness is a vital characteristic of dialogic communication.

One way to make dialogue possible is to be open to others and their ideas. Openness, however, is not enough. Dialogic communication takes place when each person perceives the other positively and productively, trusts the other as a human being, and inherently respects them. This way of being is what we focus on next.

Unconditional Positive Regard. The second characteristic of dialogic communication is a person's ability to express **unconditional positive regard**. This concept was developed by Carl Rogers (1961). *Regard* means "gaze" or a way of looking at something or someone. *Positive* implies a good, affirmative quality. *Unconditional* refers to the absence of evaluation or conditions for judgment. Together, the phrase means to look at someone with affirmation and without conditions. Rogers explained unconditional positive regard as "a caring which is not possessive, which demands no personal gratification" (p. 283). It also involves accepting people as they are; "it involves an acceptance of and a caring for the client as a *separate* person, with permission for him to have his own feelings and experiences, and to find his own meanings in them" (p. 283; emphasis in original). In essence, unconditional positive regard is a way of being toward others.

Rogers advocated the use of unconditional positive regard in therapy, but the concept also can inform everyday communication. In fact, Carl Rogers used his ideas to facilitate "international and intercultural workshops that led to his nomination for the Nobel Peace Prize" (Cissna & Anderson, 2004, p. 194). In practice outside of therapy, unconditional positive regard can take place in parental interactions with children, in education between faculty and students, and even in romantic relationships. There is a tendency in all of us to show love to the people around us by implying "I care for you *if* you behave thus and so" (Rogers, 1961, p. 283), but unconditional positive regard is about creating a context that expresses caring and warmth "with no conditions of worth attached to it" (p. 283). It is a way of stating: "I care." Dialogic communication requires both partners to take this stance and to suspend their assumptions.

In the study about dialogue from Montague (2012), one participant shared a story about a dialogic moment that she experienced with a friend who shared her struggle with an eating disorder. After sharing the story, she realized the importance of being nonjudgmental (emphasis in original):

> I think she probably knew that I wasn't going to judge her and that I would listen because I've told her about conversations that I've had with my little sister about personal teenager stuff. So, I think that she probably just felt comfortable with me because of that. Looking back, I hadn't thought about that, I had told her about conversations that I've had with my sister about personal stuff and so she probably knew that she could open up to me like my sister did, and *I wouldn't judge her or look down at her.*

The way we look at others, our perceptions, can create a barrier between ourselves and others. In this story, however, the speaker emphasizes that they were able to meet one another fully without judgment or negative perceptions. The presence of unconditional positive regard made a difference.

The more positive our perceptions become, the more likely we are to make human contact with others. Unconditional positive regard requires a person to put aside perceptions and to instead discover and listen with understanding. When this happens, a person may cultivate the ability to experience the world of others.

Empathy. Dialogic communication requires a third element: **empathy**. People need to be able to understand the perspective of others by "imagining the reality of the other" (Cissna & Anderson, 2004, p. 196). As Spiro (1993) explained, empathy is "what we feel when we see a picture that moves us"; "it is the feeling that 'I might be you' or 'I am you.'" In his work, Rogers (1961) suggested that "empathic understanding—understanding *with* a person, not *about* him—is such an effective approach that it can bring about major changes in personality" (p. 332). Empathy facilitates shared understanding, but it is an approach taken by each person: "it means to see the expressed idea and attitude from the other person's point of view, to sense how it feels to him, to achieve his frame of reference in regard to the thing he is talking about" (p. 332). Empathy essentially is about envisioning the world of another person.

The importance of empathy and its enactment, listening, is well-illustrated in *Tuesdays with Morrie*, in which Albom (1997) narrates the final months of his relationship with his college professor. For months, Mitch becomes a listener and a future messenger of Morrie's life lessons. During these dialogues, which were recorded, Morrie emphasizes the importance of listening. In one conversation, he tells Mitch: "But really listening to someone—without trying to sell them something, pick them up, and recruit them, or get some kind of status in return—how often do you get this anymore?" (p. 13). Later, Morrie strengthens his point:

He paused, then looked at me. "I'm dying, right?"

Yes.

"Why do you think it's so important for me to hear other people's problems? Don't I have enough pain and suffering of my own?

"Of course I do. But giving to other people is what makes me feel alive."

Empathy is best cultivated by experience. By living through events, we can come to grasp more fully the nature of an experience. In the process, it makes it more possible for us to understand another person's experience of a similar event. Experience enhances empathy but, ultimately, empathy is about imagination, to feel what another person feels and to thereby respond in a way that facilitates their being.

Empathy can be happening inside of us, but it is most helpful when it is communicated. In a recent article that analyzed an interaction between Carl Rogers and a client named Gloria, the researchers found that Rogers embodied his recommendation to be empathetic. In fact, he consistently displayed empathy for the patient's struggles by demonstrating his ability to comprehend Gloria's predicament (see Wickman & Campbell, 2003). For example, during the encounter, Rogers told Gloria, "Life is risky. To take the responsibility for being the person you would like to be with her is a hell of a responsibility." In two other moments, he said, respectively, "It's so damn hard to really choose something on your own" and "Sounds like a tough assignment, doesn't it?" (p. 180). In these brief interactional moments, he is displaying empathy for Gloria's struggles.

Rogers's ability to display empathy was also marked by "verbalizing what Gloria may have been thinking using her language as if he were her—and thereby again modeling 'I' messages" (p. 181). Consider how he was able to do so in these examples:

Example 1:

Rogers: But something in you says, "but I don't like it that way, not unless it is really right."
Gloria: Right

Example 2:

Rogers: You can really listen to yourself sometimes and realize, "This isn't the right feeling. This isn't—
Gloria: Mm hm
Rogers: This isn't the way I would feel, if I was doing what I really wanted to do."
Gloria: But yet many times I'll go on and do it anyway.
Rogers: Mm hm
Gloria: And say "Oh well, I'm in the situation now, I'll just remember next time."

In these two examples, Rogers is repeatedly speaking as if he were Gloria. He uses an "I" perspective to make visible to Gloria that he understands her thought process and the way she feels. In the first excerpt, she immediately agrees with the way he is positioning her perspective. In the second excerpt, she pursues the line of reasoning by adding, "I'll go on and do it anyway." In sum, Rogers is speaking in a way to display his understanding of the person's world. By speaking as if he were Gloria, he can enact his keen understanding of her thinking. The most important function of his talk, however, is to show a deep involvement in the encounter, listening to her so attentively that he can display an understanding of her world. As he explained in *On Becoming a Person*:

> If I can listen to what he can tell me, if I can understand how it seems to him, if I can see its personal meaning for him, if I can sense the emotional flavor which it has for him, then I will be releasing potent forces of change in him. (p. 332)

The communicative challenge of empathy is to listen deeply to understand another person's experience. The implications can be incredible if, as Rogers pointed out, we had the courage to listen to others in this way:

> If you really understand another person in this way. If you are willing to enter his private world and see the way life appears to him, without any attempt to make evaluative judgments, you run the risk of being changed yourself. You might see it his way, you might find yourself influenced in your attitudes or your personality. This risk of being changed is one of the most frightening prospects most of us can face. (p. 333)

For Rogers, listening with empathy was a crucial part of client-centered therapy, but it made possible human contact in a variety of other contexts. In fact, Floyd (2014) has argued that empathic listening is a form of affection in all forms of relationships. As he defined it, **empathic listening** is "the active and emotional involvement of a listener during a given interaction; an involvement that is conscious on the part of the listener but is also perceived by the speaker" (p. 6). Empathic listening demonstrates immediacy, "results in the recipient feeling better understood and validated," and invests "time and energy that implies their worth to the listener" (p. 6). In important ways, then, listening with empathy is a form of affectionate communication. This is well-exemplified in this interaction between a father (Christopher) and a 10-year-old son (Noah) who are watching nature together while camping (see Poulos, 2008, pp. 120–121):

Noah:	Matt says he is an atheist, but I don't believe it.
Christopher:	Why do you say that?
Noah:	Because you can't just believe in nothing.
Christopher:	Why not?

Noah:	(an earnest look on his face) Even nothing is something.
Christopher:	Yeah. Hmmm. What do you believe?
Noah:	Well, I believe in God, you know, but not like he's some guy up on a cloud or something. I think God just is.
Christopher:	(eyebrows raised) Wow. That's pretty cool. God is.
Noah:	(smiles slightly) Yeah.
Christopher:	So what's that mean?
Noah:	God is here. God's not away. It's here.
Christopher:	Really?
Noah:	Well, something made all of this. You know. It's like…the lake. You know it's beautiful, and it's a good place to be.
Christopher:	Right. So…God is in the lake.
Noah:	Definitely. God is in the lake.

In this moment, father and son are in a dialogic moment. Through communication, the father embodies empathic listening: he is present, responding and curious about his son's thinking and perspective, confirming his views without evaluating them as right or wrong, and sharing his energy in the moment. This is what empathic listening is about.

To summarize, empathy, or the ability to see and understand another person's perspective, is a core practice of dialogic communication. Empathy is something that happens inside of us, but it functions positively in communication when it is embodied. Then, it becomes empathic listening. Dialogue requires listening, but when speaking, people also need to be genuine and authentic.

Genuineness and Authenticity. The fourth characteristic of dialogic communication is to speak genuinely and authentically. Martin Buber (1958) proposed that human beings often treat each other as an "it." Primarily, he argued, persons use one another as instruments. We treat each other as objects to meet our purposes. He called this way of relating an **I-it relationship**. He suggested, however, that there is a way to engage with others that is more human, that breeds connection and compassion. He called this way of being in the world I-Thou. An **I-Thou relationship** involves respecting and treating another individual as a person, free from imposing on them, confirming their existence without using them as an instrument for our goals. I-Thou relationships, like dialogue, are fostered by each person's ability to speak genuinely and authentically.

In his work, Buber argued that the significant barrier to dialogue is **seeming** rather than **being**. Seeming involves keeping masks on, a façade, and pretending to act in a way that is in fact incongruent with our character. Dialogic moments, however, are fostered when the individual sheds this protective barrier, is honest with his or her experiences, and displays, as we saw in Chapter 6, congruency. Being, then, is simply "being what one really is" (Buber, 1965, p. 66). The more people move in the direction of being rather than seeming, the more they are authentic, the more likely they are to meet each other fully.

Moments of authenticity can occur at any time. In one study, for example, Whitaker (2013) interviewed people who divorced and asked them to share any examples of positive communication. Surprisingly, she found that people experienced many moments of positive communication during their divorce. In one interview, Whitaker asked one participant, "What conversations during the divorce would you consider beautiful or inspiring?" This is what the respondent shared:

> I remember shortly, it was very soon after he moved and I was dropping the boys off and he said "I need to talk to you for a minute." We went to the backroom. He said, "I had a dream about you last night." I can't remember all of the specific words, but it just made him feel good, so he kind of wrote me this letter, and it was really sweet. Like you know, "thank you for all of the time we had together." "I'm sorry it went bad, and that we didn't have the right tools to keep it going." That was really sweet. I wish I could remember everything that he said. It was overwhelming.

This story exemplifies how she connected with her ex-husband for a brief moment. She found the moment beautiful and inspiring in part because he shared what he felt. He is expressing gratitude and apologizing, and doing it with honesty. He is, if only momentarily, being real and genuine. Ultimately, every person can connect with the truth.

Our best communication comes from our core. It expresses who we are, our best self, and it emerges from a place of truth about how we think or feel. In Chinese medicine, a person's core is thought to reside slightly below the navel. Officially called Dantian, our core is the source of our life energy, or chi. When we speak genuinely and authentically, we draw from this energy, express it, and share it with another person. Communication is a form of vibration. When people make genuine contact, they can sense this energy, feel the vibration, and momentarily connect.

I defined dialogic communication and the concept of dialogue. Dialogic communication, I showed, involves listening openly, displaying empathy, embodying unconditional positive regard, and speaking authentically. When multiple individuals in a shared context enact these behaviors, they are able to create a dialogic moment—a fleeting moment of conversation in which they momentarily meet one another fully. Dialogic communication reflects our best potential and what we are capable of doing in the course of human interaction. With this theoretical understanding, we can now approach the more difficult task of actually practicing dialogic communication.

Practical Knowledge

"If you are listening to find out, then your mind is free, not committed to anything; it is very acute, sharp, alive, inquiring, curious, and therefore capable of discovery."

—KRISHNAMURTI, 1964, P. 27

Communication scholars and philosophers have shown that human beings can create beautiful conversation and transcend their differences. The first part of the chapter focused on dialogic communication. Being open, seeing others warmly without expectations or demands, developing empathy, and communicating genuinely are all part of the co-construction of dialogic moments. All of them, however, require listening. This section proposes that listening exemplifies positive communication.

Listening as Positive Communication

Listening is a vital part of healthy communication. As Bodie (2012) argued, "listening is *the* quintessential positive interpersonal communication behavior as it connotes an appreciation of and an interest in the other" (p. 109; emphasis in original). Listening has a wide range of positive outcomes. Researchers have shown the importance of "being heard" and empathic listening in personal growth (see, respectively, Myers, 2000; Myers & White, 2010). There also is significant research that shows the importance of listening in various contexts, including parenting (e.g., Duncan, Coatsworth, & Greenberg, 2009), family communication (e.g., Pluhar & Kuriloff, 2004), marital relationships (e.g., Pasupathi, Carstensen, Levenson, & Gottman, 1999), mentoring (e.g., Johnson & Ridley, 2004), and health care interaction (e.g., Suchman, Markakis, Beckman, & Frankel, 1997). Listening is simply an important part of how to communicate well across social contexts.

Communication always involves both listening and speaking. In some ways, listening is required to "do" conversation because to interact, people must respond to a previous turn of talk. Listening is an act of positive communication when it moves beyond treating the previous utterance as a set up for the next turn of talk. Instead, the speaker is interacting in a way as full meaning to the other person who is present. Listening functions positively in human interaction when the person is able to accurately reflect the experiences of the other, validate such experiences, display warm presence and involvement in the interaction, treat the other person as an equal, and maintain a non-evaluative stance. When listening is practiced in this way, it "fosters intimate interaction by enhancing feelings of being understood" (Bodie, 2012, p. 117), momentarily connects people more deeply, and creates a shared experience. Listening is an act of communication that fosters dialogic moments; it is a practice worth reflecting on, studying, and practicing.

Reflect on Listening. Listening is an opportunity to welcome new information. It involves being in a mode of observation, noticing, discovery. Listening is inherently about paying attention. The purpose of this exercise is to reflect on your ability to listen. To do so, you will perform three short activities that involve in sequence (a) listening to your self, (b) listening to a context, and (c) listening to nonverbal behaviors. The objective is to conduct each small exercise in sequence while using what researchers call thick description (see Geertz, 1973). **Thick description** is the written process of documenting one's observations and reflections. It is called thick description because it offers depth, precision, and substance in the process of describing an event, action, person, or communication event. After each short activity, the goal is to describe the experience in writing with as much detail, depth, and precision as possible. Thick description is a written record of the experience of being a keen observer of the human scene.

The first short exercise is to listen to yourself. Listening deeply to others requires each person to first develop the ability to listen to the experiences inside of them. Thich Naht Hanh (2001), for example, wrote:

> Listening is an art that we must cultivate. First you have to be able to listen to yourself before you can listen to someone else. You must not run away from yourself, but rather be very compassionate toward yourself.... Then, when you begin to understand and love yourself, you are ready to understand and love another person. (p. 61)

One way of beginning this process is to practice breathing and meditation.

To start the activity, you will first meditate for approximately five minutes to observe your thoughts, feelings, and any experiences that arise in the process. Then, you will describe with as much precision as you can the experience of listening to your self. Follow these steps:

1. Sit down in a chair at home.
2. Close your eyes.

3. Become aware of your breathing. Inhale slowly through your nose and exhale gently through your mouth.

4. Listen for five minutes to any experiences that emerge within you. To quote Kabat-Zin (1994), "Let go into full acceptance of the present moment, including how you are feeling and what you perceive to be happening. For these moments, don't try to change anything at all, just breathe and let go. Breathe and let be" (pp. 12–13). Enjoy the process of listening to your mind, to your thoughts, and emotions.

5. Open your eyes whenever you are ready to end the process.

After the meditation, write down 300 words to describe what you have just experienced. Describe what you did with as much precision and detail as you can. You may, for instance, reflect about these questions:

> What was the experience like for you?
> What thoughts emerged during the meditation?
> What memories arose during the process?
> What made you uncomfortable or comfortable?

Be thick in your descriptions of what happened during these five minutes.

For the second exercise, you will observe human interaction in a public space such as a local café, park, or museum. The objective is to listen to the context and to write any observations of what is *currently happening as you are observing it*. You may focus on a couple having a conversation, a person reading, or the ways in which people collectively move through space. Proceed in this way:

1. Find a public space.
2. Sit comfortably with a pen and paper.
3. Describe with as much detail as you can what you are seeing and observing for 10–15 minutes.
4. Provide thick descriptions of the place in which you are located, the people who are coming in and out of the space, the verbal and non-verbal behaviors that people are exhibiting, as well as anything that you are experiencing during this time.

Your only objective is to describe everything that you see and that you are experiencing with as much precision and detail as possible. After conducting the experiment, reflect on what you wrote.

The third short exercise is about listening to others with your hands. In his book *Have a Little Faith*, Mitch Albom (2009, p. 59) shares this wonderful story from a sermon delivered by his rabbi in 1958. The story captures well the importance of nonverbal communication in listening:

> A little girl came home from school with a drawing she's made in class. She danced into the kitchen, where her mother was preparing dinner.
>
> "Mom, guess what?" She squealed, waving the drawing.
>
> Her mother never looked up.
>
> "What?" she said, tending to the pots.
>
> "Guess what?" The child repeated, waving the drawing.
>
> "What?" the mother said, tending to the plates.
>
> "Mom, you're not listening."
>
> "Sweetie, yes I am."
>
> "Mom," the child said, "you're not listening with your *eyes*."

We can listen with our eyes, but as this exercise will help you see, we can also listen with our hands.

For this exercise, you need to ask someone to be part of the experience. You and this person will then practice an art that is common in China called "push hands." In this art, people face each other, make contact with their bodies, and move together to push each other off balance. For us, however, the objective will not be able to push or win, but to simply make contact and listen. To begin with push hands, you and your partner should do the following:

1. Begin by facing each other and placing each of your right foot forward and next to each other; they should be parallel to each other.
2. Raise your right elbow in front of you and both of you should make contact with the back of the right hand.
3. Place your left hand on the other person's right elbow. The other person should do the same.
4. Both of you are now connected.

To begin, move your arms and bodies together without losing contact. Do this back-and-forth movement for at least three to four consecutive minutes, listening along the way to any clue about the other person. It is in here to be completely silent; you can both close your eyes if that help your hands, listen to the other person's movements, body, and anything else that you can feel with your hands. Notice what happens when you push more strongly or when you become loose. Pay attention to the tightness in the person's arm or neck. Use your hands to capture emotional states such as degree of stress, anxiety, relaxation, openness, or vitality. Seek to capture any facet of personality. Listen with your hands as long as you can. When the time has elapsed, share what you have experienced and what you felt with your hands. After you are done, write a thick description of the experience.

Thick descriptions provide a substantive description of a person's observations. These three exercises are designed to help you reflect about the importance of listening in everyday communication. After paying attention to your own ability to listen, you can then study the experiences of others.

Study Listening. Listening is an important part of positive interpersonal communication. As argued in the chapter, listening enables communicators to transcend their differences. Scholars call these moments **interpersonal transcendence**. Essentially, interpersonal transcendence "are characterized by absorption in the unfolding conversation where participants experience a sense of discovery, creation, and a feeling of connection, or 'sharedness,' that could only be achieved via interaction" (Greene & Herbers, 2011, p. 66). From the perspective of Greene and Herbers, these are often moments of "listening in the extreme." They reflect interpersonal experiences in which people feel deeply listened to, understood, or supported. They involve a meeting of the minds and can only be experienced through the process of listening.

The purpose of this short study is to develop an understanding of the role that listening plays in interpersonal transcendence. To proceed, you will need to conduct six interviews with people that you do not know at all. Each interview should last 10–15 minutes and will focus on participants' experiences with listening and the ways in which they have experienced "transcendence." To conduct these interviews, use the following short interview schedule. Feel free to add any open-ended questions that you would like to ask:

1. What is an example in your life when you have felt deeply listened to by another person?
2. When have you felt deeply understood?
3. What is an example of a conversation in which you felt completely absorbed with the other person?

4. What is an example of a conversation in which you felt deeply connected to another person? How did listening enable this moment?
5. What compels you to listen to others?
6. What are common barriers that you experience as a listener?

These questions should get the conversation started. Consider other questions and probe as deeply as you can and listen to the responses to see what emerges. Once you have conducted the six interviews, reflect on what you have learned by considering these questions: What are the common characteristics of deep listening? What enables people to transcend their differences? What is the role of listening in interpersonal communication? After reflecting, write down three major learning points from your interviews. Then, you can use those stories to deepen your own listening practices.

Practice Listening. Listening is about paying attention, being involved, and giving voice to the other person. In his work, Rogers proposed that one effective approach to listening is to make sure to restate the other person's ideas or thoughts before continuing on. His rule for listening was simple and yet remarkably difficult. "Each person," he explained, "can speak up for himself only after he has first restated the ideas and feelings of the previous speaker accurately and to that speaker's satisfaction" (p. 332). By engaging in communication in this way, he argued, persons in conversations could reach mutual understanding.

This practice session is about deep listening. According to Thich Naht Hanh (2001), a Zen monk, author, and meditation master, **deep listening** "consists of keeping compassion alive in your heart the whole time that you are listening" (p. 62). It involves focusing on the other person, giving them a chance to express themselves as openly as they can, and to withhold from judgments and evaluations. As he wrote: "You do not listen in order to judge, criticize, or evaluate. You listen for one reason alone: to offer the other person a chance to express him- or herself" (p. 62). Deep listening is simply about being present with another person and giving them your full attention without judgment or evaluation.

The purpose of this exercise is to practice deep listening. The objective is to interview a good friend about his or her childhood before the age of 12 for one full hour. To prepare for the interview, consider these directions (based on Norkunas, 2011, p. 90).

1. Focus on the narrator's life before the age of 12. You may ask him or her about parents and grandparents.
2. Record the interview.

3. The interview should last one full hour.
4. Ask many follow-up questions to probe more deeply.
5. Help the narrator create a richly detailed portrait of his or her childhood.
6. Topics can include grandparents, parents, childhood house, inside rooms, special places inside the house, meaningful outside places, play, games, friends, and any other thing that you would like to inquire about.
7. Focus on giving voice to the other and listening to the narrator as deeply as you can.

After conducting the interview, reflect on the challenges of listening deeply. What was difficult about listening? What moments were most challenging? When did you feel most connected to the interviewee? What would you do differently in the future?

Deep listening is an art. This practice session can help you strengthen the ability to give to others the ability to express themselves. More importantly, it can help you deepen your friendship and help you become a little closer.

Summary

Listening exemplifies positive communication. By listening to others, we can give a bit of ourselves and enable others to express themselves. Listening deeply can make possible dialogic moments, foster mutual understanding, enable the growth of both individuals, and reveal our commonalities. As we saw in this chapter, listening depends on our willingness to be open to others, to listen empathetically, to express unconditional positive regard, and to speak authentically. In its truest form, listening is an act of compassion. It exemplifies the uniquely human ability to be with others and thereby functions as a moral act (see Frank, 1995). By listening to one another just a bit more, we can narrow the gap between ourselves and others, transcend our separateness, and make each other a little bit more green.

Further Reading

Albom, M. (1997). *Tuesdays with Morrie: An old man, a young man and life's greatest lesson.* New York: Doubleday.

Anderson, K., Baxter, L. A., & Cissna, K. (Eds.). (2004). *Dialogue: Theorizing difference in communication studies.* Thousand Oaks, CA: Sage.

Baker, P. (1977). *Integration of abilities: Exercises for creative growth*. New Orleans, LA: Anchorage Press.

Buber, M. (1958). *I and thou*. New York: Scribner.

Coelho, P. (2011). *Aleph*. (M. J. Costa, Trans.). New York: Random House. (Original work published 2010).

Krishnamurti, J. (1964). *Think on these things*. New York: Harper & Row.

Lionni, L. (1959). *Little blue and little yellow*. New York: Harper Collins.

Peters, J. D. (1999). *Speaking into the air: A history of the idea of communication*. Chicago: In University of Chicago Press.

Rogers, C. (1961). *On becoming a person*. Boston, MA: Houghton Mifflin.

Thich Naht Hahn. (2001). *You are here: Discovering the magic of the present moment*. Boston, MA: Shambhala.

Key Conceptual and Theoretical Terms

dialogue
dialogic moments
dialogic communication
openness
unconditional positive regard
empathy
    empathic listening
genuineness and authenticity
I-it relationship
I-Thou relationship
seeming versus being
thick description
interpersonal transcendence
deep listening

· 8 ·

POSITIVE COMMUNICATION
INFLUENCES OTHERS

Prelude

About two years ago, Dr. Arvind Singhal visited my department. Arvind is well-respected for his scholarship on the diffusion of innovation and for igniting social change across the globe with an approach called positive deviance. Arvind delivered a presentation and was then available to meet with students. At the time, the department was creating study abroad opportunities to France and India. The students who were going to India came to the session because Arvind is originally from India. At one point, he asked the students for questions. One student raised his hand and said, "Well, as you know, we're going to India. Do you have any advice for us?" Arvind paused for a second and then responded:

Absolutely. When you travel to India, you will spend countless hours on the plane before you land in New Delhi. Then, you'll be tired and exhausted. You'll enter the airport and your world will be changed by new smells, new people around you, new sights and colors. You'll get a taxi and get into it. When you sit down, you'll notice that all of the children in the area will rush towards you. They will want to talk to you, to touch your hands, to ask questions, and to interact with you. Your instinct at this moment will be to roll up your windows, to close yourself off, and to be safe. What about instead of doing that, you roll down your windows. You decide to make contact with the children, to talk to them, and let Indian culture come into your life and affect you.

Introduction

"All you can do is to alter your relationship with the world, not the world of Europe or America, but the world of your wife, your husband, your work, your home. There you can bring change, and that change moves in wider and wider circles."
—KRISHNAMURTI, 1992, P. 22

In a famous story, a woman asks Mahatma Gandhi to talk to her son about stopping to eat sugar. In response, Gandhi asked the mother to come back in a week and bring her child. The next week, and upon return, Gandhi spoke to the child and told him to stop eating sugar. And the child did. A month later, the woman came back and said: "My child has done what you asked, but why could you not have spoken to him the first time I came." "Because," said Gandhi, "a week earlier I was still eating sugar."

The most effective mode of influence is modeling. As Lockwood, Jordan, and Kunda (2002) explained, "Positive role models can inspire one by illustrating an ideal, desired self, highlighting possible achievements that one can strive for, and demonstrating the route of achieving them" (p. 854). People learn most from each other. For this reason, the way a person communicates will naturally influence people in the present and in the future. In this chapter, I propose that positive communication is influential. By definition, to influence someone is the capacity to have an effect "on the character, development, or behavior of someone" (Influence, n.d.). In this chapter, I especially wish to emphasize that every person is constantly modeling and thereby teaching others how to be—or whom to become. This is why communicating well is particularly important. To bring these ideas to life, the first major section increases your theoretical understanding of how communication influences others. The second major part of the chapter invites you to be inspiring.

Theoretical Knowledge

This section is designed to increase your theoretical understanding of how positive communication is influential. To do so, I introduce three major theoretical frameworks. The first theory is called Communication Accommodation Theory.

The theory has a long history in the field of communication and shows how people move in the direction of others or create distance, as well as how they are influenced by micro-behaviors that create connection and satisfaction. The second theory, the Positive Deviance approach, takes a larger perspective as it focuses on how individuals can influence larger systems such as communities. The theory will capture how modeling desirable behaviors in a community will create waves of influence beyond the act. Social change, however, often begins with one person. This is why I then focus on virtue ethics, a perspective that calls each of us to practice communication with character and integrity.

Communication Accommodation Theory

When people interact, there is a natural tendency to adjust verbal and non-verbal behaviors. Persons in conversations can either align their communication with those of others or seek to differentiate themselves from the other. This idea is well captured by a theory called **Communication Accommodation Theory** (henceforth CAT; Giles, Coupland, & Coupland, 1991). Basically, CAT suggests that when people want to fit in a social group, they imitate the communicative behaviors of the people around them to fit in and create similarity. When people seek distance, however, their communication will instead diverge. As Gallois, McKay, and Pittam (2005) explained, "according to CAT, speakers are motivated either to seek approval and indicate liking by bringing themselves and their interlocutors closer through their communicative moves, or alternatively, to create more social distance" (p. 233). Based on CAT, persons in conversation can either converge or diverge in the way they communicate. Convergence is used to mark similarity, liking, inclusion, and approval. Divergence, on the other hand, is used to mark difference, disapproval, uniqueness, or disagreement.

By definition, **convergence** refers to any communicative "strategy whereby individuals adapt to each other's communicative behaviors" (Giles et al., 1991, p. 7). **Divergence**, in comparison, is defined as "the way in which speakers accentuate speech and nonverbal differences between themselves and others" (p. 8). When people experience or seek (consciously or unconsciously) a need for solidarity, a degree of intimacy, or liking, their communication behavior will therefore match. Speech convergence, the authors explained, "reflects in the unmarked case, a speakers' or a group's need (often unconscious) for social integration or identification with another" (p. 18). Said simply, convergence takes place when people move in the direction of another person's way of speaking. Researchers have shown that this convergence takes place at many levels. People match one another's rate of speech, the length of utterances, the quality of pitch, the accent being spoken, the vocal patterns, the density of the information being shared, the pausing frequencies and length, the amount of self-disclosure, and even the nature of the jokes being shared.

Convergence also takes place nonverbally. In the course of interaction, people can match each other's nonverbal behaviors, including head movements, gestures, facial expressions, and so forth. Scholars in nonverbal communication call this process body synchrony. **Body synchrony** takes place when a person performs an action, gesture, or movement that is immediately subsequently matched by another person. Frequently, body synchrony involves the matching of **micro-behaviors**, small and taken-for-granted behaviors such as gaze, gestures, and body positions (see Streeck & Mehus, 2005). We know from research in this area that people imitate an incredible range of nonverbal actions such as their posture, body position, mannerisms, nonverbal emotional displays, the way they coordinate interaction, and even the quality of their movements. As Ramseyer and Tschacher (2011) explained, "Even simple body-movements, such as walking, are more synchronized in dyads with positive relationships." Overall, the research on body synchrony shows that it is evidence of positive emotion and liking between people and that synchrony fosters positiveness and quality relationship.

The principle of convergence highlights that people in interaction are momentarily and often unconsciously echoing each other's talk, body movements, or vocal patterns. To see this process in action, consider this moment between three people: Julien, Michael, and Carol. Michael and Carol have been teaching together for 17 years. Julien is a colleague who is interviewing them in front of a large audience. At one point during the interview, Michael and Carol asked the audience to jot down some notes to ground the discussion. Then, Julien initiated a conversation about a concept that Michael introduced. (The equal sign [=] is used here to note that there is almost no pause at all between what is being spoken from all three participants.)

Julien:	So, it is similar to the concept of synergy (Figure 8.1). It's like these two forces come together and = (Figure 8.2)
Michael:	= and pow! =
Julien:	= POW! = (Figure 8.3)
Michael:	= yeah =
Carol:	= Pow (Figure 8.4)

In this short moment, all three participants use the same utterance: "pow." So they each speak and match each other's verbal message; first Michael, then Julien, and third Carol. This is verbal convergence. Now, look at this moment again. This time, examine the photographs to see what happened nonverbally.

Figure 8.1. Julien (left) says "synergy".

Figure 8.2. Julien (left) says "and".

Figure 8.3. Julien (left) says "POW!".

Figure 8.4. Carol (right) says "pow".

This interaction is happening quickly. It lasts less than five seconds. During this time, however, the three interactants are producing similar gestures. Note how in Figure 8.1, all three individuals are leaning toward one another, which shows involvement and interest in the conversation. The hands also are down (see Figure 8.1). As Julien says the word "and" Michael is beginning to complete that sentence. Meanwhile, Michael's hands move upward; Julien's hand follows that same pattern instinctively (see Figure 8.2). In Figure 8.3, both of Michael's hands are faced upward and Julien's left hand is doing the same thing (the right hand cannot do it because it is holding paper). Then, Michael makes a token of agreement: "yeah." Almost immediately, and as shown in Figure 8.4, Carol performs the same gesture that Michael performed a few milliseconds earlier: both hands are raised, with palms facing upward. Together, Julien, Michael, and Carol are performing a dance: they are matching one another's words and performing similar gestures. This is what convergence is about and how people create good relationships without even knowing it.

Communication Accommodation Theory has shown the many ways in which people converge and diverge. It has emphasized that convergence can "attenuate communicative differences, bring the other person psychologically closer, accentuate shared group memberships, indicate empathy, and enhance conversational effectiveness" (Williams & Giles, 1996, p. 224). What makes CAT particularly important is that it also shows that a person's behavior can have a significant impact on whether another is receptive to them. Said differently, depending on how a person communicates, he or she may be creating divergence or convergence, liking or disliking, and can be influential or not. In short, the way communication unfolds can create a sense of satisfaction or dissatisfaction.

In interpersonal interaction, people often join the conversation with distinct social identities. They may be French or American, black or white, teacher or student, or old or young. In these situations, "people frequently categorize each other in terms of their social identities, and more often than not, this results in treatment of individuals in terms of stereotypes associated with their particular social group and can often lead to negative evaluations, misunderstandings, and even conflict" (Williams & Giles, 1996, p. 221). In their research, Williams and Giles (1996) explored retrospective accounts of intergenerational conversations to understand what ingredients made them satisfying or dissatisfying. What they found is that age between people is irrelevant. What matters is the way people communicate. Certain communication behaviors fostered dissatisfaction and certain behaviors created satisfaction.

On the side of dissatisfaction, the most frequent behaviors mentioned were "not listening, interrupting, and inattentive" (Williams & Giles, 1996, p. 233) as well as closed-mindedness. These are some examples of what participants reported about those behaviors (p. 233):

Inattention:	"He seemed a little reserved and he asked short-ended questions which made it seem like he wasn't especially interested, and there wasn't much I could do to elicit enthusiasm."
Nonlistening:	"She wasn't listening to me at all.... I got overnice with her and that made her even more angry."
Closed minded:	"He did most of the talking and did not really seem to care about what I said.... He appeared to be so closed minded and unreceptive to new ideas."

In addition to dissatisfaction, these communication behaviors reinforced the negative stereotypes related to age and made it unlikely for people to connect.

Some behaviors fostered satisfaction. These behaviors included (a) demonstrating interest and attentiveness, (b) providing emotional or instrumental support, (c) encouraging, (d) advice-giving, and (e) complimenting. One participant, for instance, illustrated the importance of these supportive behaviors: "She understands everything I said. She supported me in my thoughts because we were on the same wavelength in a way. I can talk to her about anything." The author's research also showed that "openly disclosing about one's life and circumstances" (Williams & Giles, 1996, p. 237) was critical. These positive communication behaviors thus fostered a positive climate, enabled participants to overcome the divide of the age differences, and connected more deeply.

Communication Accommodation Theory is a useful theoretical framework to understand how and why communicators converge or diverge. It functions as an important reminder that the way people communicate matters. Some behaviors, performed consciously or unconsciously, move us in the direction of others, create intimacy and liking, as well as give us the possibility of influencing others. The next section focuses on the Positive Deviance Approach to understand even more how people can influence one another.

Positive Deviance Approach

Learning takes place both consciously and unconsciously by interacting with people around us. As we saw above, we pick up others' nonverbal behaviors, respond to their interactive moves, and acquire our style of communication through interaction. We influence each other a great deal, sometimes even without our knowing. In this section, I introduce the Positive Deviance Approach to show that modeling is the most persuasive approach to influencing others.

In our everyday communication, people are constantly acting as role models. But, some people do some things more effectively than others with the same resources. This is the basic premise of the **Positive Deviance (PD) Approach**, which has been used to create social and economical change in local communities across the globe (see Singhal, 2010). The Positive Deviance Approach is grounded in the principle that "local wisdom trumps outside expertise when it comes to solving the most intractable problems" (p. 1) and that "In every community, there are individuals whose uncommon practices/ behaviors enable them to find better solutions to problems than their neighbors with access to the same resources" (Dura & Singhal, 2009, p. 2). Positive Deviance is an approach that has been used to solve salient problems around the world, including malnutrition in Vietnam, girls' trafficking in Indonesia, or child soldiers in Uganda.

The basic idea of the PD approach is to identify the individuals or groups of persons that are functioning positively with the same resources as others. As Singhal (2013) explained, "PD is premised on the belief that in every organization or community there are certain individuals or groups whose uncommon behaviors and strategies enable them to find better solutions to problems than their peers, while having access to the same resources and facing even worse challenge" (p. 143). In Vietnam, for example, the persons involved in an intervention for malnourished children realized that some children from poor families were healthy. In spite of few resources, the mothers found a way to provide healthy nutrition to their children. These mothers were thus positively deviant: they were doing something good (positive) that most mothers in the community did not do (deviant). Typically, Positive Deviance programs "focus on individuals who behave differently from the rest of the community and, in so doing, succeed where others fail" (Kim, Heerey, & Kols, 2008, p. 1413). Instead of forcing people to change their behaviors, agents of social change first study the "Positive Deviants," learn from their practices, and often showcase them in the intervention. As Singhal (2013) explained, "change is led by internal change agents who, with access to no special resources, present the social behavioral proof to their peers. If they can do it, others can too" (p. 11). Very often, the social intervention places the positive deviants center stage as role models. In Vietnam, for example, the agents led the intervention by

> creat[ing] a program whereby community members could interact with and emulate the positive deviants in their midst. Mothers, whose children were malnourished, were asked to forage for shrimp, crabs, and sweet potato green, and in the company of other mothers who taught to cook new recipes that their children ate right there. Within weeks, mothers could see their children becoming healthier. (Dura & Singhal, 2009, p. 3)

The PD approach essentially suggests that modeling healthy behavior and having others imitate it is at the heart of leading social change.

Recent research has applied the PD approach to a variety of new contexts, including education. In this context, positive communication has tangible outcomes. For example, researchers found that teachers who were the most effective in reducing dropout rates in Argentina "showed unusual respect for the students" (Singhal, 2013, p. 149) and "warmly greeted parents whenever they visited the school" (p. 149). In El Paso, Texas, Kallman (2012) found that several communicative practices were critical in leading students to academic success for learning-disabled students. These included

(a) Consistent self-affirmations and self-validations
(b) Positive messages from parents, family members, friends, peers, teachers, and mentors praising their grit and determination
(c) Clear messages received from parents to not use their disability as a crutch (p. 154)

The words of affirmation were critical to students' success. Mentors and teachers spoke in unison: "You can do anything you put your mind to," "don't be afraid to ask for help," and "surround yourself with a network of good people" (Kallman, 2012, p. 83). In short, positive communication with students has both short-term and long-term consequences.

Positive Deviance has yet to be applied to interpersonal communication. Indeed, more research is needed to identify the communication practices that truly matter in outstanding marriages, in great friendships, or in closely knit families. We know from research by Maslow (1971) that in peak marriages, couples tend to give to the relationship without holding back. They give without comparing to what the other person is doing. We also know that the first step toward marital happiness is communication and awareness (Young, 2004, p. 160). Research by Gottman (1999) also suggests that the most important element to sustain a healthy marriage is the ability to maintain a **five-to-one ratio**; every negative act is compensated by five positive acts. In a study of enduring marriages, Robinson and Blanton (1993) found that communication was critical. "Positive communication skills," the authors elaborated, "involved sharing thoughts and feelings, discussing problems together, and listening to the other's point of view" (p. 41). In the context of friendships, researchers have shown that best friends overcome the transition to college not because of proximity, but because of communication. It is self-disclosure, social support, and positive maintenance behaviors that make all the difference (see Oswald & Clark, 2003) in keeping best friends alive. In the context of family, the communicative strengths include open communication patterns, showing appreciation for one another, creating a supportive environment, and handling stress in an effective manner (DeFrain & Stinnett, 1992). Across contexts, thus, enacting the positive communication behaviors proposed in this book has tangible outcomes. When people enact those behaviors, they are positively deviant; they deviate from the norm and are able to create wonderful connections with people.

The Positive Deviance Approach is grounded in the principle that "the wisdom to solve a problem lies with ordinary people ... who have found resilient ways to achieve better outcomes" (Singhal, 2013, p. 157). The theoretical approach also is a reminder that enacting positive behaviors can be the impetus for social change and that modeling is the most persuasive form of communication. Most often, as I will now explore, change must begin with the self.

Virtue Ethics and Communication Excellence

More than 2,500 years ago, the ancient Greek philosopher Aristotle wrote on the nature of persuasion. He argued that there were three forms of persuasion: *ethos*, *pathos*, and *logos*. Ethos, he explained, was the most important form of persuasion. While **logos** emphasizes that people are persuaded by the logic of an argument and **pathos** highlights that emotional appeals such as a fear, pride, and desire can affect a person deeply, **ethos** refers to a person's moral character. A person is persuasive simply based on who they are, what they have done, and the way they act in everyday life. A person's character, or ethos, is therefore always on the line. It is cultivated by what people do on a daily basis. Their words and actions, then, are persuasive based on their character as a person, and the way they have embodied their beliefs, values, and everyday virtues.

With this understanding, Aristotle proposed a perspective on ethics called *Nicomachaean Ethics*, or simply named **virtue ethics**. As Kim (2004) explained, "Aristotle's is an ethics not of principles and rules, but of character ... proper and appropriate relations to others ... it is an ethics of self-development, and duties to oneself" (p. xiii). For Aristotle, man is capable of enacting the great virtues such as courage, compassion, and generosity. Every person has the capacity to engage in virtuous activity, that is, to be excellent. The word *virtue*, in fact, comes from the Greek word *arête*, which translates as excellence and "implies a respect for the wholeness and oneness of life" (Pirsig, 1974, p. 341). There is, in each of us, a duty to live up to that potential, to act in accordance with what is right, ethical, and just. As Comte-Sponville (2001) explained, virtue "is capacity; in the particular sense, it is human capacity, the power to be human" (p. 3).

Virtue ethics proposes that acting ethically is a duty toward the self and that a person becomes virtuous simply by engaging in virtuous activity. Seeger and Ulmer (2001), for example, explained that "the virtuous person is ethically praiseworthy not necessarily because of adherence to an external moral code, but due to some fundamental tendency to consistently act in an ethically commendable and admirable manner" (p. 370). For Aristotle, the only reward to acting ethically is to be able to live with oneself. When a person lives in accordance with virtue, he or she can experience *eudaimonia*, a state of well-being and happiness that comes as a result of "identifying one's virtues, cultivating them, and living in accordance with them" (Peterson, 2006, p. 78). Virtue ethics, therefore, is a system of ethics that calls each person to live virtuously.

Virtue ethics can easily be applied to the context of human communication. After all, "the most significant choice in interpersonal communication is to act with character" (Mirivel, 2012, p. 57). Every moment calls each person to communicate at his or her best and to draw on the great virtues to guide communication. When communicators enact these virtues, whether these are justice, mercy, humility, prudence, or temperance, they are embodying communication at its best and therefore serve as role models for others. Our sources of inspiration, in fact, often come from individuals who momentarily enact a virtue, whether it is gentleness, generosity, or love. Martin Luther King Jr., Nelson Mandela, Rosa Parks, the Little Rock Nine, or Gandhi inspire all of us to reach our best self. But virtues can also guide everyday communication. **Communication excellence**, then, is the term I use to refer to any verbal and nonverbal messages that embody a virtue in the course of human interaction. Little research has focused on this kind of positive communication, but interpersonal communication is laden with moments in which people exhibit love, tolerance, purity, or gentleness (see Mirivel, 2012).

In one study, Seeger and Ulmer (2001) featured two great examples of communication excellence in action. Their work examined the responses of two leaders to an organizational crisis. By definition, an **organizational crisis** is "a specific, unexpected, and nonroutine event or series of events that create high levels of uncertainty and simultaneously present an organization with both opportunities for and threats to its high-priority goals" (Ulmer, Sellnow,

& Seeger, 2015, p. 8). Examples of a crisis may include terrorism, violence at work, natural disasters, or product failure. Sometimes, leaders respond to a crisis by communicating unethically. For example, CEOs may diffuse responsibility, use strategic ambiguity, blame external stakeholders, or hide relevant information. On rare occasions, some leaders exhibit communication excellence. One example featured in Seeger and Ulmer's (2001) study is Aaron Feuerstein, owner and manager of Malden Mills, a textile producer (also see Ulmer, 2001). In 1995, "The plant exploded resulting in 36 injuries" (p. 371). The facility was destroyed thereby leaving many employees without a job. Immediately, however, Feuerstein communicated to the public and his stakeholder that he would "rebuild his company and to continue pay workers and provide their health benefits" (p. 371). In personal communications, Feuerstein explained that "the corporation has a responsibility to its community" (p. 372). Shortly after the fire, he immediately communicated with the community: "We're going to continue to operate in Lawrence ... we had the opportunity to run to the south many years ago. We didn't do it then and we're not going to do it now" (Milne, 1995, p. B1; cited in Seeger & Ulmer, 2001). Through his communication, Feuerstein reduced uncertainty for the community, exhibited his commitment to his employees, and responded to the crisis ethically.

Communication excellence can be done publicly, but it can be enacted in everyday interactions. Gentleness, for example, can be embodied between mentors and students. In one story, Pausch (2008) narrates this moment:

> He put his arm around me and we went for a little walk and he said: Randy, it's such a shame that people perceive you as so arrogant because it's going to limit what you're going to be able to accomplish in life. What a hell of a good way to word: you're being a jerk.

As displayed here, gentleness in communication may involve monitoring the impact of one's utterances. Courage, as we saw earlier, can be enacted in disclosing the truth. Compassion can be embodied by listening to those who are suffering. Generous communication may involve interpreting other's actions positively and monitoring the design of utterances with effect in mind. Justice can be fostered by enabling others to make informed decisions and by refusing to engage in dehumanizing practices. And mercy can be practiced by the expression of forgiveness. In sum, the great virtues can guide communicative conduct. Communication excellence is the embodiment of virtues in everyday interaction, reflects a person's capacity to be human in interpersonal communication, and can serve as a model for others (see Mirivel, 2012).

In this theoretical knowledge section, I introduced three main theoretical frameworks to show that positive communication is influential. The first theory was Communication Accommodation Theory (CAT). CAT makes visible how small choices in communication can enable convergence or divergence in interaction and can cultivate a context to overcome perceived differences. Positive communication makes this possible. The second theory is the Positive Deviance (PD) approach to social change. Based on this approach, we discovered how modeling behavior is the most influential approach to persuasion and that high-quality relationships across many contexts naturally practice positive communication behaviors. Finally, I described virtue ethics to invite you to communicate in accordance with virtues. The next section moves from theory to practice: to be influential.

Practical Knowledge

"Every communication has the power of personal survival in it. I am using survival in the sense of what one does to *matter* and to *count*."

—SATIR, 1976

Every person engaging in the process of communication is influential. An act of communication can foster contact with another or promote isolation; it can enhance understanding or suppress it; it can strengthen another person's sense of self or weaken it; it can give courage or bring out fear. In the first part of the chapter, I introduced theoretical perspectives to illustrate that positive communication is influential. This part invites you to inspire others: to communicate in a way that is exemplary.

Inspiring as Positive Communication

The verb "to inspire" means to (a) "influence, move, or guide by divine or supernatural inspiration" and (b) "to exert an animating, enlivening, or exalting influence on" (Inspire, n.d.). As Rafferty and Griffin (2004) defined it, **inspiration** is defined as "the action or power of moving the intellect or emotions" (p. 332; also see Downton, 1973). When a person inspires others, they affect them in some way through enthusiasm, motivation, encouragement, and the desire and will to overcome themselves. Inspiration simply is connection. Inspiring depends on communication: verbal and nonverbal messages that influence others.

Inspirational communication refers to any verbal and nonverbal expression of positive and encouraging messages and statements that build motivation and confidence (adapted from Rafferty & Griffin, 2004, p. 335). Inspirational communication strengthens people and fosters human development. In this sense, it is the epitome of positive communication. Inspirational communication also includes moments of communication excellence—any moment in which a person communicates with character, with integrity, and that serves as a model of what humans are positively capable of. Inspirational communication can take place in public speaking (DeFrancisco & Jensen, 1994), in organizations (Rafferty & Griffin, 2004), and in everyday interpersonal interactions at home or at work. Inspiring influences others to act well; it is a practice that is worth reflecting on, studying, and practicing.

Reflect on Inspiring. In 1997, I joined the Department of Communication Studies at the University of Northern Iowa. I enrolled in a course titled Advanced Public Speaking. My professor's name was Mr. Jensen. Although I have not seen him in person since the open house for my graduation in May 2000, I have been in contact with him in writing for the last 14 years. Today, I teach most of the courses that I took with him as an undergraduate student: interpersonal communication, communication ethics, and capstone. The only notes that I have kept from all of my courses as an undergraduate or a graduate student are the notes from the courses that I took with him. I do not know Marvin in a personal way, but his influence on me and my development as a person is simply incredible. There is no way to describe what it was like to be in his classroom. He embodied the words of Erich Fromm (1956), who wrote this about teaching: "While we teach knowledge, we are losing that teaching which is the most important one for human development: the teaching which can only be given by the simple presence of a mature, loving person." Below are several memorable communicative moments that I shared with him.

A first memorable moment took place in his office early in my coursework with him. His office door was always open, even early in the morning. I met him in his office because I received a B+ on an assignment. To be honest, I was not happy. I sat down in the chair, faced him, and tried to explain why I deserved a better grade. Then, he paused in a way that felt different from any other pause that I experienced: he was thinking, reflecting, giving time to find just the right words. He was *slowing down* the process of communication to give it space, to let it breathe. His hands folded and his demeanor joyful, he said to me: "I hope you know that in my mind, this is a very good grade." I'm sure he ıething else, but I don't remember what he said. All I remember was ıne feeling of being listened to and confirmed. From this moment on, I decided to take all of his courses without worrying at all about my grades. I just wanted to learn from him.

In class, Mr. Jensen modeled genuine teaching. I have echoes in my mind of some of the ways he would communicate with us. In response to students' questions about grades, he would say, "I will think about this in the depth of the night." And for some reason, we all believed that that's exactly what he would do: reflect on our work in the middle of the night. Often, during a lecture, he would slide in this comment, "I hope that one day we can talk about these ideas together around a fire with some wine." After hearing this statement many times in our classes, two friends and I finally gathered our courage to invite ourselves. He welcomed us into his home. And so, one night, we went to his house, drank wine and ate cheese, talked around his fireplace, and left in the depth of the night.

Marvin is still teaching me. In his letters, he reminds me of important lessons taught 14 years ago and models the life of a learner. He travels extensively, maintains valued relationships, and shares his experiences with music, art, reading, and gardening. For me, he embodies the value of good communication and continues to be a personal role model.

Many of us have had role models in our lives, people who have shown us the way and inspired us to take action or become more than we see in ourselves. The purpose of this activity is for you to reflect about the individuals who have inspired you in your life. To proceed, first reflect on these questions:

- Who are your role models?
- What individuals have inspired you?
- How do your role models communicate?
- How do they interact with you and others?
- What communicative strengths do they display?
- What words of wisdom have they shared with you?

After reflecting on these questions, write 300–500 words to describe the five main communication strengths that your role models have in common. Once you have reflected on how others have inspired you, discover yourself. Inspiring others can only unfold through you. Enthusiasm cannot be taught; it can only be experienced. Consider these questions to guide your reflection:

1. Who are you?
2. What inspires you?
3. What are your core strengths?
4. What can you give to others that is unique?
5. When do you feel most passionate? Most interesting?
6. When are you feeling most connected to people you interact with?
7. What contribution(s) are you secretly wanting to make to the world?

This activity will help you think about who and what inspires you. It may nudge you in the direction of communicating with passion. Then, you can study inspirational communication.

Study Inspiring. Communication can inspire us when we see other people speaking or acting virtuously. Few moments can be as inspiring as when people overcome conflict or transgression and move into the realm of forgiveness. Forgiveness is a virtue, but it also is often done communicatively. According to Waldron and Kelley (2008), **forgiveness communication** is an act of positive communication that has four main characteristics:

1. It is a relational process whereby harmful conduct is acknowledged by one or both partners.
2. The harmed partner extends undeserved mercy to the perceived transgressor.
3. One or both partners experience a transformation from negative to positive psychological states.
4. The meaning of the relationship is renegotiated, with the possibility of reconciliation. (p. 19)

Forgiveness communication is important in a variety of contexts, including the workplace where people work together, between siblings and family members, in romantic and non-romantic relationships, as well as in everyday encounters. In his work, Kelley (1998) studied forgiveness communication in romantic, friend, family, and work relationships to understand how they took place. He found that people expressed forgiveness in three ways. First, they expressed forgiveness *directly* by expressing it in an explicit way: "I forgive you." Second, they expressed *indirectly* by downplaying the offense such as "it was nothing." Or, they expressed it *conditionally* by making stipulations. One participant, for example, said: "I told him that I would accept his apology; however, we both knew that there was the stipulation that he stay off the booze" (p. 206). Often, the act of forgiveness functioned positively.

It restored well-being for the transgressor and/or the recipient, the relationship, as well as the moral order (Kelley, 2012). For many participants, forgiveness communication was a form of love.

The purpose of this activity is to gather narratives of forgiveness as inspiration. Your objective is to gather written stories from six participants. To proceed, use the following handout to collect the narratives (inspired by Kelley, 1998).

Forgiveness Communication

I am collecting examples of moments in people's lives when they were able to forgive someone and express forgiveness. My purpose is to understand how forgiveness unfolds in human relationships. Reflect for a moment about your life and think through any examples where forgiveness has taken place. Specifically, please share three forgiveness stories: (a) a time in which you were forgiven, (b) a time in which you forgave another person, and (c) a time in which someone else asked for forgiveness. Please share as many details as you can for each event.

After collecting these stories from six individuals, you should have about 18 stories of forgiveness communication. Now examine the stories to identify three main themes that emerged from the narratives. You may ask yourself: What stories are the most inspiring? What are the key elements of forgiveness communication? In what ways does forgiveness enable people to overcome transgression or conflict? Then, reflect on the ways in which those narratives you collected align with the findings outlined above. How do your findings match those of Kelley (1998)? After identifying the three themes, write them down and share one of your great stories with at least one person.

Practice Inspiring. Inspirational communication is about doing. It involves communicating in a way that reaches others, conveys enthusiasm and passion, and builds confidence. Any moment of communication can illustrate a person's best. This book has proposed six behaviors that function positively in human interaction. Those behaviors include (a) initiating greetings, (b) asking open-ended questions, (c) complimenting, (d) disclosing congruently and courageously, (e) encouraging, and (f) listening. From my perspective, inspiring is about enacting these behaviors in daily interactions, maximizing any opportunity for making contact with others, and avoiding missed opportunities. In his research, Gottman (1999) explained that in marriages, for example, couples have choices about whether to turn toward each other or to turn away from one another. As he explained, "turning toward versus away reflects emotional connection versus distance in the marriage" (p. 164). Couples who want to create strong relationships have to learn to change their tendency to turn toward one another. Communicating positively in everyday life functions similarly; there are opportunities to make contact and opportunities to move away from others. This practice session is about making contact. Your objective is to keep track of your ability to enact those behaviors over the course of seven days to see which behaviors you are able to perfect on a daily basis as well as identify your communicative strengths.

To proceed, start enacting these six communication strengths as often as you can. At the end of each day, take 5 to 10 minutes to reflect on your communicative performance. Use Table 8.1 to keep track of your observations. To give you a sense of how often you are performing the behavior, use a 1–5 scale to code each day. Use "1" if you performed the behavior *very frequently* throughout the day, a "2" if you have performed the behavior *frequently* throughout the day, a "3" if you performed the behavior *sometimes* throughout the day, a "4" if you *rarely* performed the behavior throughout the day, and a "5" if you *never* performed the behavior.

Table 8.1. Positive Communication Personal Assessment.

Today, I...	Day 1	Day 2	Day 3	Day 4	Day 5	Day 6	Day 7
...Initiated greetings to make contact with someone new.							
...Asked open-ended questions to discover something new about someone.							
...Complimented a person to affect their sense of self positively.							
...Disclosed to deepen a relationship.							
...Encouraged to give support to someone who needed it.							
...Listened to transcend perceived differences.							

During your reflection at the end of each day, identify your communicative strengths as well as the behaviors that you can focus on for the next day. At the end of seven days, think about your experience with these behaviors:

Which behaviors come naturally to you? Which behaviors are most difficult to enact on a daily basis? What positive communication behaviors improved the most? What are some of the challenges of communicating well? Who are you most comfortable interacting with? Consider also the ways in which you have influenced the people around you: What climate are you helping to create at work? How is your family reacting to your communication? Is the person you love closer to you or more distant? These questions can jumpstart your reflections.

Practicing positive communication is inspiring. By enacting these six behaviors, you are helping to co-create better social worlds. You are making human contact possible, nurturing relationships, strengthening people at work, or simply offering a model for your children who are learning to become adults.

Summary

Inspiring others is the pinnacle of positive communication. It rests on a person's ability to model exemplary behavior or to speak in a way that can influence a person to think or act differently. The way we learn is simple: we watch and then imitate each other. This is particularly true in human communication where a person's actions literally converge or diverge. What we do and say can become examples for others and create unknown ripple effects of influence. We do what we see and say what we hear. This is where our opportunity to make a difference lies.

Further Reading

DeFrancisco, V. L., & Jensen, M. D. (Eds.). (1994). *Women's voices in our time: Statement by American leaders*. Prospect Heights, IL: Waveland.

Fromm, E. (1956). *The art of loving*. New York: Harper Collins.

Giles, H., Coupland, J., & Coupland, N. (Eds.). (1991). *Contexts of accommodation: Studies in emotion and social interaction*. Cambridge, UK: Cambridge University Press.

Kelley, D. (1998). The communication of forgiveness. *Communication Studies, 49*(3), 255–271.

Singhal, A. (2010). Communicating what works! Applying the positive deviance approach in health communication. *Health Communication, 25*, 605–606.

Ulmer, R. R., Sellnow, T. L., & Seeger, M. W. (2015). *Effective crisis communication: Moving from crisis to opportunity*. Thousand Oaks, CA: Sage.

Williams, A., & Giles, H. (1996). Intergenerational conversations young adults' retrospective accounts. *Human Communication Research, 23*(2), 220–250.

Key Conceptual and Theoretical Terms

Communication Accommodation Theory
    convergence
    divergence
    body synchrony
micro-behaviors
Positive Deviance Approach
five-to-one ratio
virtue ethics
ethos, logos, and pathos
communication excellence
organizational crisis
inspiration
inspirational communication
forgiveness communication

· 9 ·

CONCLUSION

Prelude

My communication teacher, Mr. Jensen, once taught me this principle: "the only word that accurately describes any person is 'complex.'" Although it is often tempting to place a label or a category on a person, we often forget that every person has faced unique lived experiences that can affect the way they think or the way they behave. More importantly, every person is in progress, ever-changing, developing and growing. In every moment of living, we discover more about life, relationships, and also ourselves. The process of learning and growing as a person, in fact, is unpredictable. Some ideas that we feel we understand may take years before they are fully grasped. Our views and values may change. Extraordinary or mundane moments can alter our perspective or change our behavior. Often, I have heard students in my classes exclaim: "Oh, this person will never change." Then, I ask them: "Can you change?" Their response is always clear: "Of course."

From my vantage point, every person is a Chinese bamboo:

> Apparently, once the seed has been sown, you see nothing for about five years, apart from a tiny shoot. All the growth takes place underground, where a complex

root system reaching upward and outward is being established. Then, at the end of the fifth year, the bamboo suddenly shoots up to a height of twenty-five meters. (Coelho, 2011, p. 23)

We cannot predict when a person will shoot up in his or her own personal growth, but it may be worth remembering that even though it may not be visible, change and growth is taking place nevertheless. Every person is complex, growing like a Chinese bamboo.

Introduction

"In this world the task remains: to come closer and closer to each other in an ever-widening perimeter of communication."
—KARL JASPERS (CITED IN MCCARTY, 2009, P. 36)

Communicating positively can be learned. It is an art that requires practice, discipline, concentration, and patience. It involves developing an awareness of one's self, the drive to create a better social world, and the ability to change our behaviors for the better. As an art, it is driven by the belief that communicating well is important: it cultivates human relationships and by implication the society in which we live. Practicing positive communication keeps alive the very existence of practices that matter for the well-being of members of a relationship, family, and society. And, it sustains the core values of human culture.

I wrote this book to encourage the practice of positive communication. Learning to improve one's communication is not easy. The practice of positive communication is fraught with misconceptions, often counterintuitive, and demands both the ability to understand how complex processes of human interaction work and the ability to perform behaviors that often are more difficult to do as pressure increases. But communicating well also is rewarding. As I argued in the book, practicing positive communication cultivates the development of self, the quality of human relationships, and a healthy society. To support this argument, I introduced a model that consists of seven principles and seven behaviors of positive communication that any person can practice to improve their communication. In this conclusion, I review this model. Then, I end by emphasizing that positive communication is a creative art.

The Model of Positive Communication

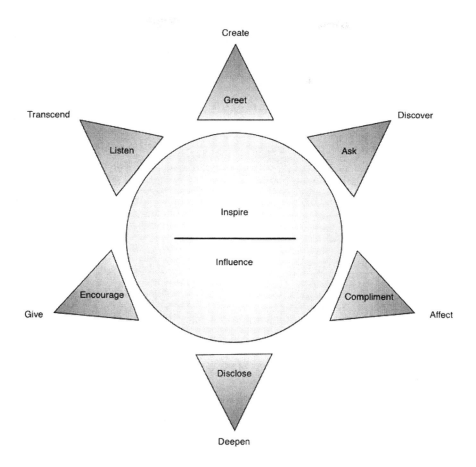

Figure 9.1. Model of Positive Communication.

Figure 9.1 summarizes the core ideas of this book, including the key verbs of the seven principles and the seven positive communication behaviors associated with each principle. Positive communication, much like the sun, gives energy and sustains life. In fact, we often describe people who are positive as "warm," "full of energy," or "beaming." I use the sun as a metaphor to encourage the practice of positive communication. Each ray in the model combines a principle and a positive communication behavior to practice. In this section, I review each ray of the model.

ˍnd Create

In Chapter 2, I introduced the principle that positive communication creates contact. Most people think that the sole purpose of communication is to exchange information. In the chapter, I showed instead that communication is a constitutive process. The way we speak and act creates our sense of self, relationships, families, and social realities. The major implication of this principle is that when you communicate, you are creating, albeit with others, the relationships you are part of.

One key function of communication is to create contact, to bring others into our world, and simultaneously acknowledge that people around us exist. This is done in the act of greeting. Think about it: How often do you greet? When do you resist greeting? When do you feel most comfortable? When do you hesitate? These are the questions that can raise your awareness about your own communication. I also emphasized in the chapter that initiating greetings is important, in part because our natural tendency is to wait for others. Greeting also is most difficult when there is a strain in the relationship or a conflict. Learning to initiate greetings in spite of tension, then, is part of what practicing positive communication is about.

Ask and Discover

The second ray of the model emphasizes that positive communication discovers the unknown. This is why people use questions in intimate and professional relationships: to discover each other. In fact, questions and answers are a fundamental structure of human interaction. Questions, depending on how they are designed, can either give or restrict freedom, lead or discover, and control or create trust with another person. I argued that the more a question is open-ended, the more it will dig beneath the surface and foster relationships.

You can reflect about how you ask questions in everyday interaction: What questions do you ask? Do you ask open-ended questions or closed-ended questions? What type of questions do you ask when you want to get to know someone? As we saw, closed-ended questions tend to limit people's response and restrict their freedom about how to respond. With open-ended questions, a person will naturally seek to discover another person more deeply and give them the freedom to provide more substantive answers. Just experiment in your own relationships and see what happens. Ask questions and you will discover the people around you.

Compliment and Affect

Communication affects the development of the self. As we saw in Chapter 4, people altercast each other, ossify one another, and their voice can become part of the voices of others. Our communication has consequences for the kind of person that we become, but it also affects the development of others. If we thought about it in this way, we could choose to emphasize the positive and to bring about the best in each other.

With this principle, I asked you to consider: Who do you compliment? Is your natural tendency to criticize or to compliment? What kinds of compliments do you share? Do you sometimes resist your impulse to compliment someone? Although all of us give and receive compliments, this third communication behavior is an invitation to do it more often and to counter our tendency to criticize others. In parenting or at work, there is a tendency in all of us to focus on what people are doing that is problematic. To compliment others requires us to see differently and to focus on the positive. When you compliment, you can affect others positively.

Disclose and Deepen

Principle four states that positive communication deepens relationship. When people talk together, they get to know one another. As a result, they create intimacy. By definition, intimacy is simply about closeness, so the main point is that communication creates closeness between people. In the chapter, I suggested that most of us fear closeness, not distance. As a result, some forms of communication are a bit scarier to engage in because they move in the direction of others. This is particularly true of the act of disclosure.

The positive communication behavior that can deepen relationships the most is to disclose. Intimacy and closeness are created as two people incrementally reveal themselves more deeply. Think again about these questions: When do you disclose? When do you not? What pieces of information do you wish you could share with others but hesitate to reveal? What forces prevent you from opening yourself up to others? The act of disclosure is liberating and often serves as an act of healing. It also is an act of courage. The stronger we are internally, the more we may be willing to be vulnerable with others. By disclosing, you can deepen your relationships.

Encourage and Give

One important human quest is to find meaning in life. As Viktor Frankl argued, we can find a meaning in life by experiencing culture, encountering someone, or by the way we respond to suffering. With Principle 5, I introduced the idea that we give to each other through the act of communication. We give each other advice, comfort, affection, and courage. But the statement also introduced the idea that a person can find a meaning in life in the act of communication itself: Communication gives meaning. This statement is true in at least two ways. First, communication literally gives meaning to our lives because our moments of interaction with others are what living is all about. Second, a person can choose to see meaning in the small and mundane moments of human connection. From this vantage point, every moment of communication is an invitation to give even more to others.

Personal success is often reached with the support of many people. Support can be provided in many ways. People can give us advice or affection when we need it. They can also give us words of encouragement. This is the fifth positive communication behavior: to encourage. In encouraging someone, we can uplift them, strengthen their spirit or their dedication, give them hope, or help them reach the next level of their personal growth. Communicating is an act of giving. This behavior requires an attentiveness to where others are: What are the people around me doing? Do they need words of encouragement? Can I say something that will make a difference in their ability to move forward or make better decisions? By observing others, you can make a contribution to others' personal growth and well-being.

Listen and Transcend

Communication transcends separateness. It bridges the natural differences between two or more persons. To make sense of this principle, I introduced the concept of dialogic communication. According to most scholars and thinkers, human beings can experience fleeting moments of genuine human connection. These moments are called dialogic moments. Dialogic moments are created when people are open, empathetic, genuine, and perceive the other with warmth. When these elements are present, people can understand each other more and create a shared field of experience.

The sixth positive communication is to listen. Observe your own conversations: How much do I talk? How much do I listen? Am I judging or evaluating the other? Am I inviting conversation by listening deeply to others? High-quality human interaction depends on the art of listening: our ability to focus on the other and to give them voice. When you listen, you can transcend human separateness and experience that we are more similar than different.

Inspire and Influence

Communication is influential. To support this principle, I first exemplified that people learn from one another in interaction by synchrony or reciprocity. Second, I provided examples to show that we learn best from the models in our lives. Any act of communication can influence people in the present and in the future. If this is true, and I believe it is, then our own communication choices can make a difference in our life and the lives of others. To quote Leo Buscaglia again, "Everybody is teaching everybody how to love at every moment."

If our communication has ripple effects of influence, then we can choose to inspire others. From my perspective, to inspire is the pinnacle of positive communication. It involves modeling the behaviors that function positively in human communication. From the perspective of this book, to inspire means to greet, ask, compliment, disclose, encourage, and listen. We know that we learn by imitating what we see and hear. With this basic conviction, every person can make the communicative choice that will foster the co-creation of better social worlds.

To summarize the model of positive communication:
When you greet, you can create contact.
When you ask, you can discover the unknown.
When you compliment, you can affect a person's sense of self.
When you disclose, you can deepen your relationships.
When you encourage, you can give support.
When you listen, you can transcend differences.
When you inspire, you can influence others.

Positive communication is about practicing behaviors that make a positive difference in our own lives and the lives of others. It involves making important choices in the small moments of human life. Social change may take place by large events and movements, but I also believe that we can improve our social worlds by making small changes in our communicative conduct. The art of positive communication can therefore begin by being aware of and then practicing these communication behaviors. But it is not the only way. You can move beyond these suggestions and express your creativity.

Communication Is a Creative Art

"The best way to prepare for a challenge is to cultivate the ability to draw on an infinite variety of responses."
—PAULO COELHO, 2011, P. 139

The most wonderful aspect of human communication is that at any moment every person has an infinite amount of possibilities about what to say. The spoken word is a creative accomplishment. Language, in fact, or the words that we have at our disposal, provides us with countless symbolic combinations. We can create new words, new expressions, new forms of humor, and more importantly for this book, we can create an act of communication that is completely unique to the circumstances facing us. Every word we use is a social invention: they reflect a person or a group's creative act. We can learn to practice communication as an art, but it is worthwhile to remember that human creativity is what makes the biggest difference in social interaction. We can initiate interaction and respond to others with options that are beyond our degree of experience, of what we've learned, or our automatic responses. I thus conclude the book by suggesting that positive communication is a creative choice.

In Chapter 2, I introduced the idea that all interactions are created by utterances that both respond to a previous move and put into motion a next-relevant response. Very often, and as we saw in Chapter 8, our utterances reflect what we have learned from others; we borrow, draw on, and imitate the vocal and bodily behaviors of others. We make them our own, use them, and thereby create interactions with other people. We develop a repertoire of responses for appropriate situations: for handling introductions and greetings, for introducing ourselves, for humor, as well as how to handle conflict. The influence from what we have seen and experienced in our lifetime is simply tremendous. As Krishnamurti (1969) wrote, "our thinking is the outcome of our own very limited experience." And yet, every person has resources in themselves that move beyond what they have learned. Creativity can be informed by experience, but it is also released from the inside.

Every word has a history but is ultimately the result of individual creativity. Our creativity is particularly noticeable in our use of humor. Every person can find a way to create utterances that will strengthen relationships, solve inter-personal conflicts, foster connection between people, or create laughter. From the perspective of this book, personal creativity is the ultimate resource needed to communicate better. Every person can create utterances that are beyond their experiences, personal tendencies, or cultural influences.

The potential to make different choices in our everyday communication is well illustrated by **Transactional Analysis**, a theory developed by Eric Berne (1966) and Harris (1967). Essentially, Transactional Analysis proposes that every person communicates on the basis of three dominant states of being. These states of being include the Parent, the Child, and the Adult.

The **Parent** is the first state of being. By definition, it is a "huge collection of recordings in the brain of unquestioned or imposed external events perceived by a person in his early years, a period which we have designated roughly as the first five years of life" (p. 40). Essentially, the child records in the "Parent" "everything that he saw his parents do and everything he heard them say" (p. 40). As Harris argued, "when we consider that the recorder is on all the time, we begin to comprehend the immense amount of data in the Parent" (p. 42). Every conversation that has taken place with the child as well as every-thing that the child has heard or seen his or her parents do is thus part of the child's personhood. All of the behaviors of the parents, the way they interact, and the words they speak ultimately become part of our Parent (p. 42).

> Remember, son, wherever you go in the world you will always find the best people are Methodists; never tell a lie; pay your bills; you are judged by the company you keep; you are a good boy if you clean your plate; waste is the original sin; you can never trust a man; you can never trust a woman; you're damned if you do and damned if you don't; you can never trust a cop; busy hands are happy hands; don't walk under ladders; do unto others as you would have them do unto you; do others in that they don't do you in.

The amount of data that becomes part of us is simply incredible and its influence is immeasurable. As Harris argued, "The significant point is that whether these rules are good or bad in the light of a reasonable ethic, they are recorded as *truth*.... It is a permanent recording. A person cannot erase it. It is available for replay throughout life" (p. 43). What we have seen our parents do and what we have heard them say thus becomes an intrinsic part of us and informs the way we interact with others. The Parent part of us helps us to process what we experience in the now and also influences what we want to say and do.

The second state of being that every person develops is a **Child**. The Child is "the recording of the *internal* events, the responses of the little person to what he sees and hears" (p. 47; emphasis in original). In other words, the Child in all of us records all of the feelings and emotions that are connected to the data in the Parent. A look from a father, a reprimand, an act of discipline, an encouragement, or a smile: all of these actions create an emotional response that also becomes part of the person. As Harris argues, however, "the predominant by-product of the frustrating, civilized process is negative feelings" (p. 48). Fortunately, there is a "bright side too. In the Child is also a vast store of positive data. In the Child reside creativity, curiosity, the desire to explore and know, the urges to touch and feel and experience, and the recordings of the glorious, pristine feelings of first discoveries" (p. 49). The Child, thus, represents the data of our inner experiences that have been accumulated over the years.

The third state of being is the **Adult**. As a child grows up, he or she begins to experience more autonomy and moves in the direction of self-actualization. The Adult is the part that develops as a result of figuring out for the self what he or she thinks, believes in, or values. As Harris explained, "Adult data accumulates as a result of the child's ability to find out for himself what is different about life from the 'taught concept' of life in his Parent and the 'felt concept' of life in his Child" (p. 51). In other words, the adult part of us is where maturity emerges. It is our attempt to ask questions and find answers for ourselves. In his work, Harris explained this well:

> One of the most important functions of the Adult is to examine the data in the Parent, to see whether or not it is true and still applicable today, and then to accept it or reject it; and to examine the Child to see whether or not the feelings there are appropriate to the present or are archaic and in response to archaic Parent data. (p. 53)

To put it simply, the Adult is the part of us that makes mature decisions, that inquires and reflects, and that seeks to find a way to act and behave in a way that might be different from what was seen or heard or that simply reacts to our fears or dreams.

Positive communication is about creating Adult responses. It is about realizing that the past does not need to shape the present or the future and that communicating well is a choice that does not depend on others. This choice can underlie all decisions as the Adult asks: "What is important here? Am I being loving?" (p. 121). Perhaps, then, these are the ultimate questions for every communicator: Am I communicating in a loving way? Am I complimenting others rather than criticizing them? Am I protecting rather than threatening a person's sense of self? Am I respectful rather than disrespectful? Is my communication aligned with my fundamental values? We can answer these questions in every communicative move we make. Our growth as persons largely depends on our ability to create communicative moves beyond our past experiences.

In one of his talks, Leo Buscaglia once said: "The healthy individual is the one with many alternatives." I think this applies to the realm of interpersonal communication. At every turn of talk, every person has an infinite amount of alternatives. Every person can invent an utterance that will nudge him or her forward in personal growth and get him or her closer to others. Being creative in the art of communication simply means to realize that we have more options than we think we have and to thereby open up the possibilities of our choices.

Communication is thus a creative art. One way to be creative is to create your own **communication ritual**. A ritual is simply something you begin to do on a daily basis with someone else. To provide an example, I'll share one of my favorite communication rituals with my son Hugo, which takes place at night: My son goes to bed. I sit next to him, ask him a few questions about his day, and then exchange kisses. As I close the door, I tell him softly that I love him and to have a good night in different languages: "I love you," "je t'aime," "ti amo," "ich liebe dich," "auf wiedersehen," "arrivederci," "bonne nuit," "ciao bambino," "won an," "assalamu alaykum abibi." Then, he looks at me and says, "I want more milk."

Summary

"While one is consciously afraid of not being loved, the real, though usually unconscious fear is that of loving."

—Fromm, 1956, p. 118

Communicating positively will make a difference. By communicating better, you will foster the co-construction of better social worlds. Relationships with others matter because we depend on each other for our sense of humanness. Relationship is, as my mentor once taught me, the essential human need. We starve for it, but it is the act of loving one another that matters even more. Physicists will cultivate our understanding of the galaxies, psychologists will improve our thinking about how the mind works, but it is communication students who will nurture our capacity for human connection. Great communicators will strengthen the human bond and will nudge us closer to our collective dream: a world at peace.

Further Reading

Coelho, P. (2011). *Aleph*. (M. J. Costa, Trans.). New York: Random House. (Original work published 2010).

Fromm, E. (1956). *The art of loving*. New York: Harper Collins.

Harris, T. A. (1967). *I'm okay—you're okay: The transactional analysis breakthrough that's changing the consciousness and behavior of people who never before felt OK about themselves*. New York: Avon Books.

McCarty, M. (2009). *How philosophy can save your life: 10 ideas that matter most*. New York: Penguin.

Key Conceptual and Theoretical Terms

Positive Communication
Transactional Analysis
    the Parent
    the Child
    the Adult
communication ritual

REFERENCES

Adler, M. J. (1983). *How to speak how to listen*. New York: Touchstone.

Agassi, A. (2009). *Open: An autobiography*. New York: Knopf.

Agne, R., & Tracy, K. (2001). "Bible babble": Naming the interactional trouble at Waco. *Discourse Studies, 3*, 269–294.

Al Falasi, H. (2007). Just say "thank you": A study of compliment responses. *Linguistics Journal, 2*(1).

Albom, M. (1997). *Tuesdays with Morrie: An old man, a young man and life's greatest lesson*. New York: Doubleday.

Albom, M. (2009). *Have a little faith: A true story*. New York: Hyperion Books.

Albrecht, T. L., & Adelman, M. B. (1987). *Communicating social support*. Thousand Oaks, CA: Sage.

Albrecht T. L., Burleson, B. R., & Sarason, I. (1992). Meaning and method in the study of communication and social support: An introduction. *Communication Research, 19*(2), 149–153.

Altman, I., & Taylor, D. (1973). *Social penetration: The development of interpersonal relationships*. New York: Holt, Rinehart and Winston.

Anderson, K., Baxter, L. A., & Cissna, K. (Eds.). (2004). *Dialogue: Theorizing difference in communication studies*. Thousand Oaks, CA: Sage.

Aune, K. S., & Wong, N. C. H. (2012). Fun with friends, pranks with partners: How we play in our closest relationships. In T. Socha & M. Pitts (Eds.), *The positive side of interpersonal communication* (pp. 143–160). New York: Peter Lang.

Austin, J. L. (1962). *How to do things with words*. Cambridge, MA: Harvard University Press.

Baack, D., Fogliasso, C., & Harris, J. (2000). The personal impact of ethical decisions: A social penetration theory. *Journal of Business Ethics, 24*(1), 39–49.

Bain, K. (2004). *What the best college teachers do.* Cambridge, MA: Harvard University Press.

Baker, P. (1977). *Integration of abilities: Exercises for creative growth.* Anchorage, AK: Anchorage Press.

Bakhtin, M. M. (1984). *Problems of Dostoevsky's poetics* (C. Emerson, Ed. and Trans.). Minneapolis: University of Minnesota Press.

Bakhtin, M. M. (1986). *Speech genres and other late essays* (No. 8). Austin: University of Texas Press.

Bakhtin, M. M. (1990). *Art and answerability: Early philosophical essays by M. M. Bakhtin.* M. Holquist & V. Liapunov (Eds.). (V. Liapunov & K. Brostrom, Trans.). Austin: University of Texas Press.

Bandura, A. (1974). *Social learning theory.* New York: General Learning Corporation.

Barnes, M. K., & Duck, S. (1994). Everyday communicative contexts for social support. In B. R. Burleson, T. L. Albrecht, & I. G. Sarason (Eds.), *Communication of social support: Messages, interactions, relationships, and community* (pp. 175–194). Thousand Oaks, CA: Sage.

Baxter, L. A., & Braithwaite, D. O. (2008). Relational dialectics theory: Crafting meaning from competing discourses. In L. A. Baxter & D. O. Braithwaite (Eds.), *Engaging theories in interpersonal communication: Multiple perspectives* (pp. 349–361). Thousand Oaks, CA: Sage.

Baxter, L. A., & Bullis, C. (1986). Turning points in developing romantic relationships. *Human Communication Research, 12*(4), 469–493.

Baxter, L. A. & DeGooyer, D., Jr. (2001). Perceived aesthetic characteristics of interpersonal conversations. *Southern Communication Journal, 67,* 1–18.

Baxter, L. A., & Montgomery, B. M. (1996). *Relating: Dialogues and dialectics.* New York: Guilford Press.

Baxter, L. A., & Montgomery, B. M. (1998). A guide to dialectical approaches to studying personal relationships. In B. M. Montgomery & L. A. Baxter (Eds.), *Dialectical approaches to studying personal relationships* (pp. 3–17). Mahwah, NJ: Erlbaum.

Baxter, L. A., Norwood, K. M., & Nebel, S. (2012). Aesthetic relating. In T. Socha & M. Pitts (Eds.), *The positive side of interpersonal communication* (pp. 19–38). New York: Peter Lang.

Bergen, M. K., Suter, E. A., & Daas, K. L. (2006). About as solid as a fish net: Symbolic construction of a legitimate parental identity for nonbiological lesbian mothers. *The Journal of Family Communication, 6*(3), 201–220.

Berne, E. (1966). *Games people play: The psychology of human relationships.* New York: Grove Press.

Bernstein–Yamashiro, B. (2004). Learning relationships: Teacher–student connections, learning, and identity in high school. *New Directions for Youth Development, 103,* 55–70.

Blum-Kulka, S. (1997). *Dinner talk: Cultural patterns of sociability and socialization in family discourse.* Mahwah, NJ: Erlbaum.

Blumstein, P. (2001). The production of selves in personal relationships. In J. O'Brien & P. Kollock (Eds.), *The production of reality: Essays and readings on social interaction* (3rd ed.). Thousand Oaks, CA: Pine Forge Press.

Bodie, G. D. (2012). Listening as positive communication. In T. Socha & M. Pitts (Eds.), *The positive side of interpersonal communication* (pp. 109–125). New York: Peter Lang.

Briede, B. (2006). Dialogue in the context of intercultural competence. *Kalbų Studijos*, 8, 58–63.

Brown, B. (2012). *Daring greatly: How the courage to be vulnerable transforms the way we live, love, parent, and lead.* New York: Penguin.

Brown, P., & Levinson, S. C. (1978). Universals in language usage: Politeness phenomena. In E. N. Goody (Ed.), *Questions and politeness: Strategies in social interaction* (pp. 56–310). Cambridge, UK: Cambridge University Press.

Buber, M. (1958). *I and thou.* New York: Scribner.

Buber, M. (1965). *Between man and man.* New York: Routledge.

Burleson, B. R. (1982). The development of comforting communication skills in childhood and adolescence. *Child Development, 53*, 1578–1588.

Burleson, B., & MacGeorge, E. (2002). Supportive communication. In M. K. Knapp & J. A. Daly (Eds.), *Handbook of interpersonal communication.* Thousand Oaks, CA: Sage.

Burnett, P. C. (2002). Teacher praise and feedback and students' perceptions of the classroom environment. *Educational Psychology, 22*(1), 5–16.

Buscaglia, L. (1982). *Living, loving, and learning.* Thorofare, NJ: Charles B. Slack.

Buscaglia, L. (1989). *Papa, my father.* Thorofare, NJ: SLACK.

Buttny, R. (1987). Sequence and practical reasoning in accounts episodes. *Communication Quarterly, 35*(1), 67–83.

Cain, R. (1991). Disclosure and secrecy among gay men in the United States and Canada: A shift in views. *Journal of the History of Sexuality, 2*, 25–45.

Cameron, D. (2001). *Working with spoken discourse.* London: Sage.

Caplan, S. E., & Samter, W. (1999). The role of facework in younger and older adults' evaluations of social support messages. *Communication Quarterly, 47*(3), 245–264.

Carns, M. R., & Carns, A. (2006). A review of the professional literature concerning the consistency of the definition and application of Adlerian encouragement. In S. Slavik & J. Carson (Eds.), *Readings in the Theory of Individual Psychology* (pp. 277–296). New York: Taylor & Francis.

Cegala, D. J. (1981). Interaction involvement: A cognitive dimension of communicative competence. *Communication Education, 30*(2), 109–121.

Cissna, K. N., & Anderson, R. (1998). Theorizing about dialogic moments: The Buber-Rogers position and postmodern themes. *Communication Theory, 8*(1), 63–104.

Cissna, K. N., & Anderson, R. (2004). Public dialogue and intellectual history: Hearing multiple voices. In K. Anderson, L. A. Baxter, & K. Cissna (Eds.), *Dialogue: Theorizing difference in communication studies* (pp. 193–208). Thousand Oaks, CA: Sage.

Coelho, P. (1993). *The alchemist.* (P. Coelho & A. R. Clarke, Trans.). New York: Harper Collins. (Original work published 1988).

Coelho, P. (2007). *The witch of Portobello.* (M. J. Costa, Trans.). New York: Harper Collins. (Original work published 2006).

Coelho, P. (2011). *Aleph.* (M. J. Costa, Trans.). New York: Random House. (Original work published 2010).

Comte-Sponville, A. (2001). *A small treatise on the great virtues: The uses of philosophy in everyday life.* (C. Temerson, Trans.). New York: Henry Holt & Co. (Original work published 1996).

Cooper, K. (2013). Stories of communication excellence between physicians and patients. (Unpublished Master's thesis.) University of Arkansas at Little Rock.

Corbin, S. D. (2003). Interactional problems with "did you" questions and responses. In. P. J. Glenn, C. D. LeBaron, & J. Mandelbaum (Eds.), *Studies in language and social interaction: In honor of Robert Hopper* (pp. 163–173). Mahwah, NJ: Erlbaum.

Coupland, J. (Ed.). (2000). *Small talk*. New York: Longman.

Craig, R. T. (1999). Communication theory as a field. *Communication Theory, 9*, 119–161.

Craig, R. T. (2006). Communication as a practice. In G. J. Shepherd, J. St. John, & T. Striphas (Eds.), *Communication as…: Perspectives on theory* (pp. 38–47). Thousand Oaks, CA: Sage.

Craig, R. T., & Sanusi, E. (2003). "So what do you guys *think?*": Think talk and process in student-led classroom discussions. In P. J. Glenn, C. D. LeBaron, & J. Mandelbaum (Eds.), *Studies in language and social interaction: In honor of Robert Hopper* (pp. 103–118). Mahwah, NJ: Lawrence Erlbaum.

Cronen, V. E. (1998). Communication theory for the twenty-first century: Cleaning up the wreckage of the psychology project. In J. S. Trent (Ed.), *Communication: Views from the helm for the 21st century* (pp. 18–38). Boston: Allyn and Bacon.

Csikszentmihalyi, M. (1990). *Flow: The psychology of optimal experience*. New York: Harper Collins.

Cupach, W. R., & Spitzberg, B. H. (Eds.). (2007). *The dark side of interpersonal communication*. Mahwah, NJ: Lawrence Erlbaum.

Cutrona, C. E., Russell, D. W., & Gardener, K. A. (2005). The relationship enhancement model of social support. In T. A. Revenson, K. Kayser, & G. Bodenmann (Eds.), *Couples coping with stress: Emerging perspectives on dyadic coping* (pp. 73–95). Washington, DC: American Psychological Association.

Cooke, P. & Eckstein, D. (2012). The seven methods of encouragement for couples. In D. Eckstein (Ed.), *The couple's match book* (pp. 12–29). Bloomington, IN: Trafford Publishing.

Dailey, R. M., Lee, C. M., & Spitzberg, B. H. (2007). Communicate aggression: Toward a more interactional view of psychological abuse. In W. R. Cupach & B. H. Spitzberg (Eds.), *The dark side of interpersonal communication* (pp. 297–326). Mahwah, NJ: Lawrence Erlbaum.

Dallimore, E. J., Hertenstein, J. H., & Platt, M. B. (2004). Classroom participation and discussion effectiveness: Student-generated strategies. *Communication Education, 53*(1).

Daly, J. A. (2011). Personality and interpersonal communication. In M. L. Knapp & J. A. Daly (Eds.), *The Sage handbook of interpersonal communication* (pp. 131–168). Thousand Oaks, CA: Sage.

DeFrain, J., & Stinnett, N. (1992). Building on the inherent strengths of families: A positive approach for family psychologists and counselors. *Topics in Family Psychology and Counseling, 1*(1), 15–26.

DeFrancisco, V. L., & Jensen, M. D. (Eds.). (1994). *Women's voices in our time: Statement by American leaders*. Prospect Heights, IL: Waveland.

de Saint-Exupéry, A. (2000). *The little prince*. (R. Howard, Trans.). Orlando, FL: Harcourt. (Original work published 1943).

DeVito, J. A. (1986). Teaching as relational development. *New Directions for Teaching and Learning, 1986*(26), 51–59.

Dindia, K. (1996). Going into and coming out of the closet: The dialectics of stigma disclosure. In B. M. Montgomery & L. A. Baxter (Eds.), *Dialectical approaches to studying personal relationships* (pp. 83–109). Mahwah, NJ: Lawrence Erlbaum.

Dindia, K. (2000). Sex differences in self-disclosure, reciprocity of self-disclosure, and self-disclosure and liking: Three meta-analyses reviewed. In S. Petronio (Ed.), *Balancing the secrets of private disclosures* (pp. 21–36). Mahwah, NJ: Erlbaum.

Dindia, K., & Tieu, T. (1996). *The process of self-disclosure of homosexual identity.* Paper presented at the Speech Communication Association Convention, San Diego, CA.

Dinkmeyer, D., & Eckstein, D. (1996). *Leadership by encouragement.* Boca Raton, FL: St. Lucie Press.

Downton, J. V. (1973). *Rebel leadership: Commitment and charisma in the revolutionary process.* New York: Free Press.

Drew, P. (1992). Contested evidence in courtroom cross-examination: The case of a trial for rape. In P. Drew & J. Heritage (Eds.), *Talk at work: Interaction in institutional settings* (pp. 470–520). Cambridge: Cambridge University Press.

Drew, P., & Heritage, J. (Eds.). (1992). *Talk at work: Interaction in institutional settings.* Cambridge UK: Cambridge University Press.

Dreyfus, H. L., & Rabinow, P. (1982). *Michel Foucault: Beyond structuralism and hermeneutics.* Chicago, IL: University of Chicago Press.

du Pré, A. (2002). Accomplishing the impossible: Talking about body and soul and mind during a medical visit. *Health Communication, 14*(1), 1–21.

Duncan, L. G., Coatsworth, J. D., & Greenberg, M. T. (2009). A model of mindful parenting: Implications for parent–child relationships and prevention research. *Clinical Child and Family Psychology Review, 12*(3), 255–270.

Dura, L., & Singhal, A. (2009). Utilitzing a positive deviance approach to reduce girls' trafficking in Indonesia. *Journal of Creative Communications, 4*(1), 1–17.

Duranti, A. (1997). Universal and culture-specific properties of greetings. *Journal of Linguistic Anthropology, 7*, 63–97.

Dweck, C. (2006). *Mindset: The new psychology of success.* New York: Random House.

Dwyer, L-L., Nordenfelt, L., & Ternestedt, B-M. (2008). Three nursing home residents speak about meaning at the end of life. *Nursing Ethics, 15*, 97–109.

Eckstein, D. (2012). *The couple's match book: Lighting, rekindling, or extinguishing the flame.* Bloomington, IN: Trafford Publishing.

Eckstein, D., & Cooke, P. (2005). The seven methods of encouragement for couples. *The Family Journal, 13*(3), 342–350.

Edelman, G. M. (2004). *Wider than the sky: The phenomenal gift of consciousness.* New Haven, CT: Yale University Press.

Fairclough, N. (2003). *Analyzing discourse: Textual analysis for social research.* New York: Routledge.

Firth, R. (1972). Verbal and bodily rituals of greeting and parting. In J. S. La Fontaine (Ed.), *The interpretation of ritual: Essays in honour of A. I. Richards* (pp. 1–38). London: Tavistock.

Fitch, K. L., & Sanders, R. E. (Eds.). (2005). *Handbook of language and social interaction*. Mahwah, NJ: Erlbaum.

Floyd, K. (2002). *Communicating affection: Interpersonal behavior and social context*. Cambridge, UK: Cambridge University Press.

Floyd, K. (2014). Empathic listening as an expression of interpersonal affection. *International Journal of Listening, 28*(1), 1–12.

Floyd, K., & Deiss, D. M. (2012). Better health, better lives: The bright side of affection. In T. Socha & M. Pitts (Eds.), *The positive side of interpersonal communication* (pp. 127–142). New York: Peter Lang.

Floyd, K., & Morman, M. T. (2000). Affection received from fathers as a predictor of men's affection with their own sons: Tests of the modeling and compensation hypotheses. *Communication Monographs, 67*(4), 347–361.

Floyd, K., & Morman, M. T. (2003). Human affection exchange: Affectionate communication in father-son relationships. *The Journal of Social Psychology, 143*(5), 599–612.

Foucault, M. (1999). *Discourse and truth: The practice of parrhesia: Six lectures given at the University of California at Berkeley, Oct.–Nov. 1983*. (J. Pearson, Ed.). Retrieved from http://www.foucault.info/documents

Frank, A. W. (1995). *The wounded storyteller: Body, illness, and ethics*. Chicago, IL: University of Chicago Press.

Frankl, V. (1984). *Man's search for meaning*. New York: Washington Square Press.

Fredrickson, B. (2013). Your phone vs. your heart. *New York Times*. Retrieved from http://www.nytimes.com/2013/03/24/opinion/sunday/your-phone-vs-your-heart.html?_r=0

Fromm, E. (1956). *The art of loving*. New York: Harper Collins.

Freire, P. (1970). *Pedagogy of the oppressed* (M. B. Ramos, Trans.). New York: Bloomsbury Academic. (Original work published 1968).

Gabriel, M., & Goldberg, E. (Directors). (1995). *Pocahontas* [Motion picture]. United States: Disney.

Gadamer, H. G. (1989). *Truth and method* (J. Weinsheimer & D. G. Marshall, Trans.). New York: Crossroad.

Gallois, C., McKay, S., & Pittam, J. (2005). Intergroup communication and identity: Intercultural, organizational, and health communication. In K. L. Fitch & R. E. Sanders (Eds.), *Handbook of language and social interaction* (pp. 231–252). Mahwah, NJ: Erlbaum.

Gallwey, W. T. (2008). *The inner game of tennis: The classic guide to the mental side of peak performance*. New York: Random House.

Geertz, C. (1973). *The interpretation of cultures*. New York: Basic Books.

Gerstenberg, A. (1941). *Overtones: A play in one act*. Philadelphia, PA: D. McKay.

Gibbs, J. L., Ellison, N. B., & Heino, R. D. (2006). Self-presentation in online personals: The role of anticipated future interaction, self-disclosure, and perceived success in Internet dating. *Communication Research, 33*(2), 152–177.

Gilbert, E. (2009). *Elizabeth Gilbert: Your elusive creative genius*. Retrieved from http://www.ted.com/talks/elizabeth_gilbert_on_genius.html

Giles, H., Coupland, J., & Coupland, N. (Eds.). (1991). *Contexts of accommodation: Studies in emotion and social interaction*. Cambridge, UK: Cambridge University Press.

Giles, H., & Ogay, T. (2007). Communication accommodation theory. In B. B. Whaley & W. Samter (Eds.), *Explaining communication: Contemporary theories and exemplars* (pp. 325–343). Mahwah, NJ: Erlbaum.

Gill, T. V. (2005). Patient "demand" for medical interventions: Exerting pressure for an offer in a primary care clinic visit. *Research on Language and Social Interaction, 38*(4), 451–479.

Glenn, P., LeBaron, C., & Mandelbaum, J. (Eds.). (2003). *Studies in language and social interaction: In honor of Robert Hopper.* Mahwah, NJ: Lowrence Erlbaum.

Goldsmith, D. J., & Fitch, K. (1997). The normative context of advice as social support. *Human Communication Research, 23*(4), 454–476.

Golish, T. D. (2003). Stepfamily communication strengths. *Human Communication Research, 29*(1), 41–80.

Golish, T., & Caughlin, J. (2002). "I'd rather not talk about it": Adolescents' and young adults' use of topic avoidance in stepfamilies. *Journal of Applied Communication Research, 30*(1), 78–106.

Gordon, R. D. (1985). Dimensions of peak communication experiences: An exploratory study. *Psychological Reports, 57,* 824–826.

Gottman, J. M. (1994). *What predicts divorce?: The relationship between marital processes and marital outcomes.* Mahwah, NJ: Lowrence Erlbaum.

Gottman, J. M. (1999). *The marriage clinic: A scientifically-based marital therapy.* New York: Norton.

Greene, J. O., & Herbers, L. E. (2011). Conditions of interpersonal transcendence. *The Intl. Journal of Listening, 25*(1–2), 66–84.

Hamilton, H. E. (1998). Reported speech and survivor identity in online bone marrow transplantation narratives. *Journal of Sociolinguistics, 2*(1), 53–67.

Harris, T. (1967). *I'm ok, you're ok.* New York: Harper Collins.

Heath, C. (2002). Demonstrative suffering: The gestural (re)embodiment of symptoms. *Journal of Communication, 52,* 597–616.

Hemingway, E. (1964). *A moveable feast.* New York: Scribner.

Heritage, J. (1984). *Garfinkel and ethnomethodology.* New York: Polity Press.

Heritage, J. C. (2003). Designing questions and setting agendas in the news interview. In P. J. Glenn, C. D. LeBaron, & J. Mandelbaum (Eds.), *Studies in language and social interaction: In honor of Robert Hopper* (pp. 57–90). Mahwah, NJ: Erlbaum.

Holladay, S. J. (2002). "Have fun while you can," "You're only as old as you feel," and "Don't ever get old!": An examination of memorable messages about aging. *Journal of Communication, 52*(4), 681–697.

Holmes, J. (1986). Compliments and compliment responses in New Zealand English. *Anthropological Linguistics, 28,* 485–508.

Holmes, J. (2000). Doing collegiality and keeping control at work: Small talk in government departments. In J. Coupland (Ed.), *Small talk* (pp. 32–61). New York: Pearson.

Holmes, J. (2003). Small talk at work: Potential problems for workers with an intellectual disability. *Research on Language and Social Interaction, 36*(1), 65–84.

Holmes, J., & Fillary, R. (2000). Handling small talk at work: Challenges for workers with intellectual disabilities. *International Journal of Disability, Development and Education, 47*(3), 273–291.

Holmes, J., & Marra, M. (2004). Relational practice in the workplace: Women's talk or gendered discourse? *Language in Society, 33*(03), 377–398.

Holmes, J., & Stubbe, M. (2003). *Power and politeness in the workplace: A sociolinguistic analysis of talk at work*. London: Longman.

Holt, E. (1996). Reporting on talk: The use of direct reported speech in conversation. *Research on Language and Social Interaction, 29*, 219–245.

Holt, E., & Clift, R. (Eds.). (2007). *Reporting talk: Reported speech in interaction*. Cambridge, UK: Cambridge University Press.

Hoppe - Nagao, A., & Ting - Toomey, S. (2002). Relational dialectics and management strategies in marital couples. *Southern Journal of Communication, 67*(2), 142–159.

Hopper, R., & Drummond, K. (1992). Accomplishing interpersonal relationship: The telephone openings of strangers and intimates. *Western Journal of Communication, 56*(3), 185–199.

Hutchby, I., & Wooffitt, R. (1998). *Conversation analysis: Principles, practices, and applications*. Malden, MA: Polity Press.

Hyams, J. (1979). *Zen in the martial arts*. New York: J. P. Tarcher.

Influence. (n.d.). In Merriam-Webster.com. Retrieved May 8, 2011, from http://www.merriam-webster.com/dictionary/influence.

IMD. (2012, August 22). *Usain Bolt's return to IMD*. Retrieved from http://www.youtube.com/watch?v=aH8yNcbJJws

Isaacs, W. (1994). Team learning. In P. Senge, A. Kleiner, C. Roberts, R. B. Ross, & B. J. Smith (Eds.), *The fifth discipline fieldbook: Strategies and tools for building a learning organization* (pp. 357–444). New York: Doubleday.

Jackson, P., Osborne, B. M., Walsh, F., (Producers), & Jackson, P. (Director). (2002). *Lord of the rings: The two towers* [Motion picture]. United States: New Line Cinema.

Johnson, W. B., & Ridley, C. R. (2004). *The elements of mentoring*. New York: Palgrave.

Judge, T. A., & Bono, J. E. (2000). Five-factor model of personality and transformational leadership. *Journal of Applied Psychology, 85*(5), 751.

Kabat-Zinn, J. (1994). *Wherever you go, there you are: Mindfulness meditation in everyday life*. New York: Hyperion.

Kallman, D. I. (2012). *Life without boundaries: A positive deviance inquiry of communication behaviors that influence academic success of learning-disabled university students*. Unpublished master's thesis, the University of Texas at El Paso, El Paso, TX.

Kassing, J. W., & Pappas, M. E. (2007). "Champions are built in the off season": An exploration of high school coaches' memorable messages. *Human Communication, 10*(4), 537–546.

Kehily, M. J., & Nayak, A. (1997). "Lads and laughter": Humour and the production of heterosexual hierarchies. *Gender and Education, 9*(1), 69–88.

Kelley, D. (1998). The communication of forgiveness. *Communication Studies, 49*(3), 255–271.

Kelley, D. L. (2012). Forgiveness as restoration: The search for well-being, reconciliation, and relational justice. In T. Socha & M. Pitts (Eds.), *The positive side of interpersonal communication* (pp. 193–210). New York: Peter Lang.

Kelley, D. L., & Sequeira, D. L. (1997). Understanding family functioning in a changing America. *Communication Studies, 48*(2), 93–108.

Kim, H-K. (2004). Introduction. In Aristotle, *Nicomachean ethics* (pp. xi–xix). New York: Barnes & Noble.

Kim, Y. M., Heerey, M., & Kols, A. (2008). Factors that enable nurse-patient communication in a family planning context: A positive deviance study. *International Journal of Nursing Studies, 45*, 1411–1421.

Kinnaird, L. (2009). The best greeting: "We've been waiting for you." *Creative Nursing, 15*(3), 136–138.

Knapp, M. L., & Daly, J. A. (Eds.). (2011). *The Sage handbook of interpersonal communication.* Thousand Oaks, CA: Sage.

Knapp, M. L., Stohl, C, & Reardon, K. K. (1981). "Memorable" messages. *Journal of Communication, 31*(4), 27–41.

Kohn, P. M. (1996). On coping adaptively with daily hassles. In M. Zeidner & N. S. Endler (Eds.), *Handbook of coping* (pp. 181–201). New York: John Wiley & Sons.

Krakauer, J. (2007). *Into the wild.* New York: Anchor Books.

Kremer-Sadlik, T., & Kim, J. L. (2007). Lessons from sports: Children's socialization to values through family interaction during sports activities. *Discourse & Society, 18*(1), 35–52.

Krishnamurti, J. (1964). *Think on these things.* New York: Harper & Row.

Krishnamurti, J. (1992). *On relationship.* New York: Harper Collins.

Kurtz, G. (Producer) & Kershner, I. (Director). *Star wars episode V: The empire strikes back* [Motion Picture]. United States: 20th Century Fox.

Laver, J. (1975). Communicative functions of phatic communion. In A. Kendon, M. R. Harris, & M. R. Key (Eds.), *Organization of behavior in face-to-face interaction* (pp. 215–240). Chicago, IL: Aldine.

Lebacqz, K. (1985). *Professional ethics: Power and paradox.* Nashville, TN: Abingdon Press.

Lewis, C. S. (1960). *The four loves.* New York: Harcourt Brace.

Li, C-S., Lin, Y-F. Lai, Y-L. Eckstein, D., Mullener, B. (2011). A research study of student teachers implementing classroom encouragement. *International Journal of Academic Research, 3*, 893–898.

Linell, P. (1998). *Approaching dialogue: Talk, interaction and contexts in dialogical perspectives* (Vol. 3). Amsterdam, Netherlands: John Benjamins.

Lionni, L. (1959). *Little blue and little yellow.* New York: Harper Collins.

Lockwood, P., Jordan, C. H., & Kunda, Z. (2002). Motivation by positive or negative role models: Regulatory focus determines who best will inspire us. *Journal of Personality and Social Psychology, 83*, 854–864.

MacGeorge, E., Feng, B., & Burleson, B. R. (2011). Supportive communication. In M. L. Knapp & J. A. Daly (Eds.), *The Sage handbook of interpersonal communication* (pp. 317–354). Thousand Oaks, CA: Sage.

MacGeorge, E., Feng, B., Wildum, K., & Doherty, E. (2012). Supportive communication: A positive response to negative life events. In T. Socha & M. Pitts (Eds.), *The positive side of interpersonal communication* (pp. 211–228). New York: Peter Lang.

Mandelbaum, J. (2008). Conversation analysis theory: A descriptive approach to interpersonal communication. In L. A. Baxter & D. Braithwaite (Eds.), *Engaging theories in interpersonal communication* (pp. 175–188). Thousand Oaks, CA: Sage.

Maslow, A. (1968). *Toward a psychology of being* (2nd ed.). New York: Van Nostrand.

Maslow, A. (1971). *The farther reaches of human nature.* New York: Penguin.

Matsuura, H. (2004). Compliment-giving behavior in American English and Japanese. *JALT JOURNAL, 26*(2), 147–170.

McCarty, M. (2009). *How philosophy can save your life: 10 ideas that matter most.* New York: Penguin.

McCroskey, J. C. (1984). Communication competence. The elusive construct. In R. N. Bostrom (Ed.), *Competence in communication: A multidisciplinary approach* (pp. 259–268). Beverly Hills, CA: Sage.

McCroskey, J. C., & Richmond, V. P. (2000). Applying reciprocity and accommodation theories to supervisor/subordinate communication. *Journal of Applied Communication Research, 28,* 278–289.

Mead, G. H. (1934). *Mind, self, and society from the perspective of a social behaviorist.* Chicago, IL: University of Chicago.

Meryn, S. (1998). Improving doctor-patient communication: Not an option, but a necessity. *BMJ: British Medical Journal, 316,* 1922.

Millman, D. (2000). *Way of the peaceful warrior: A book that changes lives.* Novato, CA: New World Library.

Milne, J. (1995, December 15). Mill owner says he'll pay workers for month. *Boston Globe,* B1, 50.

Mirivel, J. C. (2008). The physical examination in cosmetic surgery: Communication strategies to promote the desirability of surgery. *Health communication, 23*(2), 153–170.

Mirivel, J. C. (2012). Communication excellence. In T. J. Socha & M. J. Pitts (Eds.), *The positive side of interpersonal communication* (pp. 57–72). New York: Peter Lang.

Mirivel, J. C., & Thombre, A. (2010). Surviving online: An analysis of how burn survivors recover from life crises. *Southern Communication Journal, 75*(3), 232–254.

Mirivel, J. C., & Tracy, K. (2005). Premeeting talk: An organizationally crucial form of talk. *Research on Language and Social Interaction, 38,* 1–34.

Mishler, E. G. (1984). *The discourse of medicine: Dialectics of medical interviews.* Norwood, NJ: Ablex.

Mongeau, P. A., & Henningsen, M. (2008). Stage theories of relationship development. In L. A. Baxter & D. O. Braithwaite (Eds.), *Engaging theories in interpersonal communication: Multiple perspectives* (pp. 363–375). Thousand Oaks, CA: Sage.

Montague, R. R. (2012). Genuine dialogue: Relational accounts of moments of meeting. *Western Journal of Communication, 76*(4), 397–416.

Montgomery, B. M. (1981). The form and function of quality communication in marriage. *Family Relations,* 21–30.

Morgan, W., & Wilson, S. R. (2007). Explaining child abuse as a lack of safe ground. In W. R. Cupach & B. H. Spitzberg (Eds.), *The dark side of interpersonal communication* (pp. 327–362). Mahwah, NJ: Lawrence Erlbaum.

Morman, M. T., & Floyd, K. (1999). Affectional communication between fathers and young adult sons: Individual- and relational-level correlates. *Communication Studies, 50*(4), 294–309.

Morman, M. T., & Floyd, K. (2002). A "changing culture of fatherhood": Effects on affectional communication, closeness, and satisfaction in men's relationships with their fathers and their sons. *Western Journal of Communication*, 66(4), 395–411.

Mueller, C. M., & Dweck, C. S. (1998). Praise for intelligence can undermine children's motivation and performance. *Journal of Personality and Social Psychology*, 75(1), 33.

Myers, S. (2000). Empathic listening: Reports on the experience of being heard. *Journal of Humanistic Psychology*, 40(2), 148–173.

Myers, S. A., & White, C. M. (2010). The abiding nature of empathic connections: A 10-year follow-up study. *Journal of Humanistic Psychology*, 50(1), 77–95.

Nepo, M. (2007). *Facing the lion, being the lion: Finding inner courage where it lives.* San Francisco: Conari Press.

Norkunas, M. (2011). Teaching to listen: Listening exercises and self-reflexive journals. *Oral History Review*, 38(1), 63–108.

Nussbaum, J. F., Miller-Day, M., & Fisher, C. L. (2012). "Holding each other all night long": Communicating intimacy in older adulthood. In T. Socha & M. Pitts (Eds.), *The positive side of interpersonal communication* (pp. 91–108). New York: Peter Lang.

Oswald, D. L., & Clark, E. M. (2003). Best friends forever?: High school best friendships and the transition to college. *Personal Relationships*, 10(2), 187–196.

Pasupathi, M., Carstensen, L. L., Levenson, R. W., & Gottman, J. M. (1999). Responsive listening in long-married couples: A psycholinguistic perspective. *Journal of Nonverbal Behavior*, 23(2), 173–193.

Pausch, R. (2008). *The last lecture.* New York: Hyperion.

Pearce, W. B. (1989). *Communication and the human condition.* Carbondale, IL: Southern Illinois University Press.

Pearce, W. B. (1994). *Interpersonal communication: Making social worlds.* New York: Harper Collins.

Pearce, W. B. (2007). *Making social worlds: A communication perspective.* Malden, MA: Blackwell.

Pearce, W. B., & Cronen, V. E. (1980). *Communication, action and meaning: The creation of social realities.* New York: Praeger.

Pearce, W. B., Harris, L. M., & Cronen, V.E. (1981). The coordinated management of meaning: Human communication in a new key. In C. Wilder-Mott & J. Weakland (Eds.), *Rigor and imagination: Essays from the legacy of Gregory Bateson* (pp. 149–194). New York: Praeger.

Pearce, W. B., & Pearce, K. A. (2000a). Extending the theory of the coordinated management of meaning (CMM) through a community dialogue process. *Communication Theory*, 10(4), 405–423.

Pearce, W. B., & Pearce, K. A. (2000b). Combining passions and abilities: Toward dialogic virtuosity. *Southern Communication Journal*, 65, 161–175.

Pennebaker, J. W. (1990). *Opening up: The healing powers of confiding in others.* New York: William Morrow.

Pennebaker, J. W. (1997). Writing about emotional experiences as a therapeutic process. *Psychological Science*, 8(3), 162–166.

Peters, J. D. (1999). *Speaking into the air: A history of the idea of communication.* Chicago, IL: University of Chicago Press.

Peterson, C. (2006). Strengths of character and happiness: Introduction to special issue. *Journal of Happiness Studies, 7*(3), 289–291.

Peterson, C., & Seligman, M. E. (2004). *Character strengths and virtues: A handbook and classification.* New York: Oxford University Press.

Petronio, S. (1991). Communication boundary management: A theoretical model of managing disclosure of private information between marital couples. *Communication Theory, 1*(4), 311–335.

Petronio, S. (2002). *Boundaries of privacy: Dialectics of disclosure.* Albany, NY: State University of New York Press.

Petronio, S., & Durham, W. T. (2008). Communication privacy management theory: Significance for interpersonal communication. In L. A. Baxter & D. O. Braithwaite (Eds.), *Engaging theories in interpersonal communication: Multiple perspectives* (pp. 309–322). Thousand Oaks, CA: Sage.

Petronio, S., Reeder, H. M., Hecht, M. L., & Mon't Ros-Mendoza, T. (1996). Disclosure of sexual abuse by children and adolescents. *Journal of Applied Communication Research, 24,* 181–199.

Pirsig, R. (1974). *Zen and the art of motorcycle maintenance: An inquiry into values.* New York: Bantam Books.

Pitsounis, N. D., & Dixon, P. N. (1988). Encouragement versus praise: Improving productivity of the mentally retarded. *Individual Psychology: Journal of Adlerian Theory, Research & Practice, 44,* 507–512.

Platt, F. W., & Gordon, G. H. (1999). *Field guide to the difficult patient interview.* Philadelphia, PA: Lippincott Williams & Wilkins.

Pluhar, E. I., & Kuriloff, P. (2004). What really matters in family communication about sexuality? A qualitative analysis of affect and style among African American mothers and adolescent daughters. *Sex Education, 4*(3), 303–321.

Pomerantz, A. (1978). Compliment responses: Notes on the cooperation of multiple constraints. In J. Schenkein (Ed.), *Studies in the organization of conversation interaction* (pp. 79–112). New York: Academic Press.

Pomerantz, A. (1988). Constructing skepticism: Four devices used to engender the audience's skepticism. *Research on Language and Social Interaction, 22*(1–2), 293–313.

Poulos, C. N. (2008). Accidental dialogue. *Communication Theory, 18*(1), 117–138.

Pratkanis, A. R., & Gliner, M. D. (2004). And when shall a little child lead them? Evidence for an altercasting theory of source credibility. *Current Psychology, 23*(4), 279–304.

Prather, H. (1970). *Notes to myself: My struggle to become a person.* New York: Bantam.

Pressfield, S. (2002). *The war of art: Break through the blocks and win your inner creative battles.* New York: Black Irish Entertainment.

Pugh, L. (2009). *Lewis Pugh swims the North Pole.* Retrieved from http://www.youtube.com/watch?v=HALd9FY5-VQ

Rafferty, A. E., & Griffin, M. A. (2004). Dimensions of transformational leadership: Conceptual and empirical extensions. *The Leadership Quarterly, 15*(3), 329–354.

Ramseyer, F., & Tschacher, W. (2011). Nonverbal synchrony in psychotherapy: Coordinated body movement reflects relationship quality and outcome. *Journal of Consulting and Clinical Psychology, 79,* 284–295.

Robinson, J. D. (2003). An interactional structure of medical activities during acute visits and its implications for patients' participation. *Health Communication, 15,* 27–59.

Robinson, L. C., & Blanton, P. W. (1993). Marital strengths in enduring marriages. *Family Relations, 42,* 38–45.

Rogers, C. (1961). *On becoming a person.* Boston, MA: Houghton Mifflin.

Rom, S. M., & Guerrero, L. K. (2001). The effects of nonverbal immediacy and verbal person centeredness in the emotional support process. *Human Communication Research, 27*(4), 567–596.

Roloff, M. E., & Chiles, B. W. (2011). Interpersonal conflict: Recent trends. In M. L. Knapp & J. A. Daly (Eds.), *The Sage handbook of interpersonal communication* (pp. 423–442). Thousand Oaks, CA: Sage.

Roter, D. L. (1984). Patient question asking in physician-patient interaction. *Health Psychology, 3*(5), 395.

Roter, D. L., & McNeilis, K. S. (2003). The nature of the therapeutic relationship and the assessment of its discourse in routine medical visits. In T. L. Thompson, A. M. Dorsey, K. I. Miller, & R. Parrott (Eds.), *Handbook of health communication* (pp. 121–140). Mahwah, NJ: Erlbaum.

Sabourin, T. C., & Stamp, G. H. (1995). Communication and the experience of dialectical tensions in family life: An examination of abusive and nonabusive families. *Communications Monographs, 62*(3), 213–242.

Sacks, H. (1992). *Lectures on conversation* (2nd vol.; G. Jefferson, Ed.). Cambridge, MA: Blackwell.

Satir, V. (1976). *Making contact.* Ann Arbor, MI: University of Michigan Press.

Schegloff, E. A. (1968). Sequencing in conversational openings. *American Anthropologist, 70,* 1075–1095.

Schegloff, E. A. (1988). From interview to confrontation: Observations of the Bush/Rather encounter. *Research on Language and Social Interaction, 22*(1–4), 215–240.

Searle, J. R. (1969). *Speech acts: An essay in the philosophy of language.* London: Cambridge University Press.

Searle, J. R. (1979). *Expression and meaning: Studies in the theory of speech acts.* New York: Cambridge University Press.

Seeger, M. W. (1997). *Organizational communication ethics: Decisions and dilemmas.* Cresskill, NJ: Hampton Press.

Seeger, M. W., & Ulmer, R. R. (2001). Virtuous responses to organizational crisis: Aaron Feuerstein and Milt Colt. *Journal of Business Ethics, 31*(4), 369–376.

Seinfeld, J. (n.d.). *Michael Richards: It's bubbly time, Jerry.* Retrieved from http://comediansincarsgettingcoffee.com/michael-richards-its-bubbly-time-jerry

Seligman, M. E. (2002). *Authentic happiness: Using the new positive psychology to realize your potential for lasting fulfillment.* New York: Free Press.

Seligman, M. E. P. (2011). *Flourish: A visionary new understanding of happiness and well-being.* New York: Free Press.

Sharf, B. F., & Vanderford, M. L. (2003). Illness narratives and the social construction of health. In T. L. Thompson, A. M. Dorsey, K. I. Miller, & R. Parrott (Eds.), *Handbook of health communication* (pp. 9–34). Mahwah, NJ: Lowrence Erlbaum.

Shekerjian, D. (1990). *Uncommon genius: Tracing the creative impulse with forty winners of the MacArthur award.* New York: Penguin.

Sifianou, M. (2001). Oh! How appropriate!. Compliments and politeness. In A. Bayrtaktaroglou & M. Sifianou (Eds.), *Linguistic politeness: The case of Greece and Turkey* (pp. 391–430). Amsterdam, Netherlands: John Benjamins.

Singhal, A. (2010). Communicating what works! Applying the positive deviance approach in health communication. *Health Communication, 25,* 605–606.

Singhal, A. (2013). Transforming education from the inside out. In R. Hiemstra & P. Carre (Eds.), *A feast of learning: International perspectives on adult education and change.* Charlotte, NC: Information Age.

Smith, S., & Butler Ellis, J. (2001). Memorable messages as guides to self-assessment of behavior: An initial investigation. *Communication Monographs, 68*(2), 154–168.

Socha, T. J., & Pitts, M. J. (Eds.). (2012a). *The positive side of interpersonal communication.* New York: Peter Lang.

Socha, T. J., & Pitts, M. J. (2012b). Positive interpersonal communication as child's play. In T. J. Socha & M. J. Pitts (Eds.), *The positive side of interpersonal communication* (pp. 323–324). New York: Peter Lang.

Spiro, H. M. (1993). What is empathy and can it be taught? In H. M. Spiro, M. McCrea Curnen, E. Peschel, & D. St-James (Eds.), *Empathy and the practice of medicine: Beyond pills and the scalpel* (pp. 7–14). New Haven, CT: Yale University Press.

Spitzberg, B. H. (1983). Communication competence as knowledge, skill, and impression. *Communication Education, 32*(3), 323–329.

Spitzberg, B. H., & Cupach, W. R. (2011). Interpersonal skills. In M. L. Knapp & J. A. Daly (Eds.), *The Sage handbook of interpersonal communication* (pp. 481–524). Thousand Oaks, CA: Sage.

Stewart, C. J., & Cash, W. B. (2011). *Interviewing: Principles and practices* (13th ed.). Dubuque, IA: McGraw Hill.

Stewart, J., Zediker, K. E., & Black, L. (2004). Relationships among philosophies of dialogue. In K. Anderson, L. A. Baxter, & K. Cissna (Eds.), *Dialogue: Theorizing difference in communication studies* (pp. 21–38). Thousand Oaks, CA: Sage.

Stockett, K. (2009). *The help.* New York: Berkley Books.

Streeck, J., Goodwin, C., & LeBaron, C. (2011). *Embodied interaction: Language and body in the material world.* Cambridge, UK: Cambridge University Press.

Streeck, J., & Mehus, S. (2005). Microethnography: The study of practices. In K. L. Fitch & R. E. Sanders (Eds.), *Handbook of language and social interaction* (pp. 381–404). Mahwah, NJ: Erlbaum.

Suchman, A. L., Markakis, K., Beckman, H. B., & Frankel, R. (1997). A model of empathic communication in the medical interview. *JAMA, 277*(8), 678–682.

Szekely, L. (writer). (2007). *Louis C. K.: Shameless* (An HBO comedy special). New York, NY: Home Box Office, Inc.

Tannen, D. (1989). Interpreting interruption in conversation. In B. Music, R. Graczyk, & 1st initial Wiltshire (Eds.), *Papers from the 25th annual regional meeting of the Chicago Linguistic Society part two: Parasession on language in context* (pp. 266–287). Chicago, IL: Chicago Linguistic Society.

Telaumbanua, Y. (2012). Complimenting as a conversation opener: A strategy in teaching English speaking proficiency. *Journal Polingua, 1*(1), 32–38.

Thich Naht Hahn. (2001). *You are here: Discovering the magic of the present moment.* Boston, MA: Shambhala.

Thompson, T. L., Dorsey, A. M., Miller, K. I., & Parrott, R. (Eds.). (2003). *Handbook of health communication.* Mahwah, NJ: Erlbaum.

Tillich, P. (1952). *The courage to be.* New Haven, CT: Yale University Press.

Tracy, K. (2002). *Everyday talk: Building and reflecting identities.* New York: Guilford Press.

Tracy, K. (2008). "Reasonable Hostility": Situation-appropriate face-attack. *Journal of Politeness Research. Language, Behaviour, Culture, 4*(2), 169–191.

Tracy, K., & Tracy, S. J. (1998). Rudeness at 911: Reconceptualizing face and face-attack. *Human Communication Research, 25,* 225–251.

Trees, A. R., Kerssen-Griep, J., & Hess, J. A. (2009). Earning influence by communicating respect: Facework's contributions to effective instructional feedback. *Communication Education, 58*(3), 397–416.

Ulmer, R. R. (2001). Effective crisis management through established stakeholder relationships: Malden Mills as a case study. *Management Communication Quarterly, 14*(4), 590–615.

Ulmer, R. R., Sellnow, T. L., & Seeger, M. W. (2015). *Effective crisis communication: Moving from crisis to opportunity.* Thousand Oaks, CA: Sage.

Vaillant, G. E. (2012). *Triumphs of experience: The men of the Harvard Grant Study.* Cambridge, MA: Belknap Press of Harvard University Press.

van Dijk, T. A. (Ed.). (1997). *Discourse as social interaction* (Vol. 2). Thousand Oaks, CA: Sage.

Vangelisti, A. L. (2007). Communicating hurt. In W. R. Cupach & B. H. Spitzberg (Eds.), *The dark side of interpersonal communication* (pp. 121–142). Mahwah, NJ: Lowrence Erlbaum.

VanLear, C. A. (1987). The formation of social relationships A longitudinal study of social penetration. *Human Communication Research, 13*(3), 299–322.

Wade, S. (2011). *The George Carlin letters: The permanent courtship of Sally Wade.* New York: Gallery Books.

Waldron, V. R., & Kelley, D. L. (2008). *Communicating forgiveness.* Thousand Oaks, CA: Sage.

Waldvogel, J. (2007). Greetings and closings in workplace email. *Journal of Computer-Mediated Communication, 12*(2), 456–477.

Watts, A. (1966). *The book: On the taboo against knowing who you are.* New York: Random House.

Weinstein, E. A., & Deutschberger, P. (1963). Some dimensions of altercasting. *Sociometry, 26,* 456–466.

Whitaker, R. (2013). Positive communication during divorce. (Unpublished master's thesis) University of Arkansas at Little Rock.

Wickman, S. A., & Campbell, C. (2003). An analysis of how Carl Rogers enacted client-centered conversation with Gloria. *Journal of Counseling and Development, 81*(2), 178–184.

Wieland, M. (1995). Complimenting behavior in French/American cross-cultural dinner conversations. *French Review, 68,* 796–812.

Wiggins, S. (2001). Construction and action in food evaluation: Conversational data. *Journal of Language and Social Psychology, 20*(4), 445–463.

Wiggins, S. (2002). Talking with your mouth full: Gustatory mmms and the embodiment of pleasure. *Research on Language and Social Interaction, 35*(3), 311–336.

Williams, A., & Giles, H. (1996). Intergenerational conversations young adults' retrospective accounts. *Human Communication Research, 23*(2), 220–250.

Wolfson, N., & Manes, J. (1980). The compliment as a social strategy. *Research on Language & Social Interaction, 13*(3), 391–410.

Wood, J. T. (1994). Engendered identities: Shaping voice and mind through gender. In D. Vocate (Ed.), *Intrapersonal communication: Different voices, different minds* (pp.145–167). Mahwah, NJ: Lowrence Erlbaum.

Wood, L. A., & Kroger, R. O. (2000). *Doing discourse analysis: Methods for studying action in talk and text.* Thousand Oaks, CA: Sage.

Worthington, E. L., & Drinkard, D. T. (2000). Promoting reconciliation through psychoeducational and therapeutic interventions. *Journal of Marital and Family Therapy, 26*(1), 93–101.

Wright, K. (2002). Social support within an on-line cancer community: An assessment of emotional support, perceptions of advantages and disadvantages, and motives for using the community from a communication perspective. *Journal of Applied Communication Research, 30*(3), 195–209.

Wright, K. B., & Bell, S. B. (2003). Health-related support groups on the Internet: Linking empirical findings to social support and computer-mediated communication theory. *Journal of Health Psychology, 8*(1), 39–54.

Yoshimura, S. (2007). The communication of revenge: On the viciousness, virtues, and vitality of vengeful behavior in interpersonal relationships. In W. R. Cupach & B. H. Spitzberg (Eds.), *The dark side of interpersonal communication* (pp. 277–296). Mahwah, NJ: Lowrence Erlbaum.

Young, M. A. (2004). Healthy relationships: Where's the research? *The Family Journal, 12*(2), 159–162.

Youssouf, I. A., Grimshaw, A. D., & Bird, C. S. (1976). Greetings in the desert. *American Ethnologist, 3*(4), 797–824.

INDEX

abusive versus non-abusive couples 66–67, 72

account and accounting 42, 49

adjacency pair 25–27

advice 100–104, 144
  aging 102
  athletics 103
  dilemmas 103

aesthetic relating 85

affectionate communication 105–108, 126

afterlife 39

Albom, M. 130, 138, 141, 177

Altman, I. 81, 95, 171

altercasting 60–63

Anderson, R. 126, 129–130, 141, 177, 179, 190

asking 9, 11, 39, 43, 47, 52–55, 154
  functions of 52–53

Austin, J. L. 19, 20, 171, 176

authoring 67, 70

autonomy-connection dialectical tension 82

Bakhtin, M. M. 59, 67–68, 70, 76, 172

Baxter, L. A. 4, 5, 81, 85, 92, 95, 135, 171–173, 175, 180, 182, 184

beautiful communication 85, 128

Blumstein, P. 59, 63, 66, 76, 172

Bodie, G. D. 129–130, 172

body synchrony 140

boundary coordination 82

Buber, M. 118–119, 127–128, 136, 173

Burleson, B. R. 3, 99, 104, 115, 171–173, 179

Buscaglia, L. 100, 107, 115, 165, 169, 173

Cissna, K. N. 120, 123–124, 135, 171, 173, 184

closed-ended questions 11, 40–44, 46, 52–53, 55, 162

Coelho, P. 35, 56, 136, 160, 166, 170, 173

comforting communication 104–105
  high person-centered comforting
    messages 105

communication 18
     as constitutive 18
     as transmission 18
Communication Accommodation Theory
     139, 143–144
Communication Boundary Management
     Theory 82–84
communication competence 3, 31, 122
communication excellence 148–149
communication ritual 169
complaint 66–67, 122
compliment 71
complimenting 9, 71–76, 109, 144, 154, 168
     functions of 72
     effort versus intelligence 74–75
     outcome versus process 75
Comte-Sponville, A. 11, 88, 94, 148, 173
congruence 85
congruent disclosure 85–88
convergence 139–141, 143, 150
Conversation Analysis 25
     principles of 25–29
constitutive view of communication 11,
     18–19, 27
Cooke, P. 110, 113–114, 174–175
coordinated management of meaning
     theory 37–39
coordination 38
Corbin, S. D. 48–49, 174
Coupland, J. 22, 33, 139, 156, 174, 176–177
couple identity work 66
courage 88
courageous disclosure 88–90
Craig, R. T. 7, 9, 13, 18, 20, 34, 174
criticism 66–67, 72–73
cross-cultural interaction 73
Csikszentmihalyi, M. 4, 16, 34, 174
culture 17, 33, 73
Cupach, W. R. 3, 13, 174, 180, 184–186

Dantian 128
deep listening 134–135
dialogic communication 120, 119–129, 164
dialogue 119, 122, 127
     seeming versus being 127

disclosing 9, 84, 89–93, 144, 149, 163
     functions of 90–91
disclosure 81–90
     avoidance of 83
     coming-out 89
     congruence 85–88
     courage 88–90
     gratitude 94
     relationship-protection 83
     self-protection 83
divergence 139
Dweck, C. 74–76, 175, 181

Eckstein, D. 109–111, 113–114,
     174–175, 179
education 31, 52, 72, 100, 109, 123, 146
emotional support 104
     effective 104
empathic listening 126–127
empathy 43, 105, 124–126
encouragement 102, 109–114, 164
encouraging 111–115
     functions of 111–112
episodes 39
esteem support 108–110
ethos 147
eudaimonia 148

family communication 59–60, 64–65, 83–84,
     90, 107, 147, 153
father-son relationship 19, 25, 51, 64,
     100–101, 107–108, 126–127
field of experience 5, 118, 164
five-to-one ratio 72, 146
Floyd, K. 105, 107, 115, 126, 176, 191
forgiveness communication 149, 153–154
Foucault, M. 19, 88, 175–176
Frankl, V. 98, 115, 164, 176
Fromm, E. 6, 13, 117, 151, 156,
     169–170, 176

Gallois, C. 139, 176
Gallwey, W. T. 57–58, 76, 176
Giles, H. 139, 143–144, 156, 176–177, 186
Gottman, J. M. 72, 129, 146, 154, 177, 181

gratitude 93–94
greeting/greetings 9, 16–17, 24, 30–34, 162
    functions of 20–21, 30–31

Harris, T. A. 58, 76, 167–168, 170, 177
Heritage, J. 27, 44–47, 52, 56, 175, 177
Holmes, J. 22–23, 61, 69, 72, 177–178
I-it relationship 127
I-thou relationship 127
inspiration 150
inspiring 9, 150–156
    functions of 150–151
inspirational communication 151
instrumental support 100–104
intergenerational communication 143–144
interpersonal communication
    (not capitalized) 4–5
Interpersonal Communication
    (capitalized) 2
interpersonal skills 3
interpersonal transcendence 133–134
intertextuality 67–71
intertextualization 67
interview 32, 44–48, 54, 92, 110, 114,
    134–135

Jensen, M. 1, 74, 151–152, 156, 159, 174

Kelley, D. 4, 84, 153–154, 156, 178–179,
    185
Knapp, M. L. 2, 13, 100, 102, 115, 173–174,
    179, 183–184
Krishnamurti, J. 2, 24, 34, 97, 118, 120, 129,
    136, 138, 166, 179

language 19, 24, 31, 33, 59–60, 66–68,
    166
Language and Social Interaction
    (capitalized) 3
learning 6, 52, 71–72, 75–76, 90, 97, 117,
    144, 146, 159–160, 162
listening 9, 12, 121–124, 126, 129–135
    functions of 129–130, 154
logos 147
logotherapy 98

MacGeorge, E. 3, 4, 99, 100, 104, 108, 111,
    115, 173
Maslow, A. 35, 56, 71, 76, 111, 146, 180
Mead, G. H. 59, 180
medicine 42, 128
medical interaction 41–44
memorable messages 72, 100, 102–104
micro-behaviors 140
Model of Positive Communication 8,
    161, 165
Montague, R. R. 122–123, 180
Montgomery, B. M. 81, 95, 122, 172,
    175, 180

news interviews 44–48
nonverbal immediacy 105

open-ended questions 11, 40–48, 51–53,
    55–56, 133
openness 83–84, 89–90, 120, 122, 133
openness-closedness dialectic tension 82
organizational crisis 148
ossification 59, 63–67

parental communication 1, 36, 58–60,
    64–65, 75, 83–84, 103, 107, 109,
    119, 123, 167–168
parrhesia 88
pathos 147
peak communication 50, 53–56
Pearce, W. B. 37–39, 56, 120, 181
Pennebaker, J. W. 84, 91, 181–182
persuasion 147, 150
    as modeling 138–139, 144, 146–147,
    150
Petronio, S. 82–83, 91, 95, 175, 182
Pitts, M. 4, 7, 13, 171–172, 176, 179,
    180–181, 184
positive communication 5–7, 9, 10, 12, 146,
    160, 165
Positive Deviance Approach 139, 144–147,
    150
Poulos, C. N. 121, 126, 182
practical knowledge 6, 29, 52, 71, 90,
    111, 129, 150

pragmatic meaning 19
Prather, H. 80, 90, 95, 182
privacy rules 82–83, 95
progression choice 71

question(s) 39, 45
    did you questions 48–50
    consequences of 52–53

race 51, 121
regression choice 71
Relational Dialectics Theory 81–82
    contradiction 82
    dialectical tensions 82
reported speech 68–70
    direct reported speech 68
    indirect reported speech 68
retrospective interview technique 92
Rogers, C. 85–86, 95, 118, 120, 123–126,
    134, 136, 173, 183, 185

Sacks, H. 17, 24–25, 34, 36, 56, 183
Satir, V. 6, 13, 34, 71, 85, 87, 150, 183
Schegloff, E. 4, 25, 30, 183
Searle, J. R. 19, 30, 183
Seeger, M. W. 88, 148–149, 156, 183, 185
self-actualization 71, 168
self-disclosure 47, 80–81, 83, 90–91, 94, 140,
    147
Seligman, M. E. 4, 94, 95, 182–183
semantic meaning 19
Singhal, A. 137, 145–147, 156, 175, 184
Socha, T. J. 4, 7, 13, 171–172, 176, 178, 179,
    180–181, 184
Social Penetration Theory 81
    depth of disclosure 81
    breadth of disclosure 81
social support 11, 98–99, 108, 110–111,
    147
speech act 20, 24–25, 27, 31, 38–39, 53,
    71–72, 98, 109–111, 112, 115
Speech Act Theory 11, 19–25, 38
Spitzberg, B. H. 3, 5, 13, 174, 180, 184–186
stepfamily communication 83–83

supportive communication 99–100, 108,
    110–111, 115
Symbolic Interactionism 11, 59–60, 63,
    71, 76
syntactic meaning 19

Taylor, D. 81, 95, 171
theoretical knowledge 6–7, 10, 17, 37, 59,
    80, 98, 118, 138
Thich Naht Hahn 130, 134, 136, 185
thick description 130–131, 133
Tracy, K. ix, 3–4, 20, 22, 59, 171, 180, 185
transactional analysis 167
transmission model of communication 18
turning point 92–93

Ulmer, R. R. ix, 148–149, 156, 183, 185
unconditional positive regard 123–124,
    128, 135
utterance 18
    as context-shaped and context-
        renewing 27–29

Vaillant, G. 1, 13, 185
virtue ethics 147–150
voice of the lifeworld 43

Williams, A. 143–144, 156, 182, 186
workplace interaction 22–23, 30, 49–50,
    62, 69, 72, 81